Falling Open
in a World
Falling Apart

EARLY ENDORSEMENTS FOR

Falling Open in a World Falling Apart

"As this wise book eloquently reminds us, awakened living involves the boundless embrace of our precious, messy human experience in all its subtlety and complexity—the pain as well as the laughter, the confusion as well as the clarity—without either identifying with it or pushing it away. This unconditional openness is not a practice, it's our natural state, our inherently awake true nature, the timeless presence that welcomes reality just as it is because it is essentially not separate from whatever arises. Amoda Maa has it right—embodied awakening is the seamless marriage of form and emptiness, human and transcendent, vulnerable and indestructible, which meet right here and now—as you!"

—**Stephan Bodian**, teacher, author of *Meditation for Dummies*, *Wake Up Now*, and *Beyond Mindfulness*

"The invitation to fall open and to embrace what appears to be falling apart has always been a vital part of the lived awakening experience. And now that the world is shaking and—dare I say it—in the process of transformation, there is an urgency to the task at hand. Amoda speaks to this directly, and stirs the heart. Her voice is eloquent and precise—a rich and extraordinarily valuable contribution to the current zeitgeist. I cannot recommend her—and this, her latest book—highly enough."

—**Miranda Macpherson**, spiritual teacher and author of *The Way of Grace*

"Such a timely book! Amoda's clarity of writing makes the universal inner wisdom relevant and accessible to the seeker in these troubled times."

—**Ondrea Levine**, author of *The Healing I Took Birth For*, co-author with Stephen Levine of *Embracing the Beloved.*

"I love that Amoda Maa includes and works with our humanness, rather than attempting to ignore or bypass the messiness and difficulties of everyday life. But she doesn't get entangled in the mess either. Instead, Amoda invites a falling open into 'the groundless ground of unbroken presence,' the openness that allows everything to be as it is. Paradoxically, this is exactly where genuine transformation happens. There is a gentle tenderness in this book. The words come from the heart, from clear seeing, and from the openness that the book invites the reader to discover. Amoda encourages 'listening to the deepest truth in you, listening to that which is prior to narrative and prior to reactivity, listening to the silence within—and then moving from this silence. Or not moving at all.' *Falling Open* is a beautiful book that I very highly recommend. As Amoda says, 'This book is a transmission. Do not read it. Feel it.' Yes!"

—**Joan Tollifson**, author of *Death: The End of Self-Improvement* and *Nothing to Grasp*

Falling Open in a World Falling Apart

Amoda Maa

Larson Publications
Burdett, New York

ISBN-10: 1-936012-92-8 | ISBN-13: 978-1-936012-92-3
eBook: 978-1-936012-93-0

Library of Congress Control Number: 2020942742
Publisher's Cataloging-In-Publication Data
(Prepared by The Donohue Group, Inc.)
Names: Jeevan, Amoda Maa, author.
Title: Falling open in a world falling apart / Amoda Maa.
Description: Burdett, New York : Larson Publications, [2020]
Identifiers: ISBN 9781936012923 | ISBN 1936012928 | ISBN
    9781936012930 (ebook)
Subjects: LCSH: Awareness--Religious aspects. | Religious awakening. |
    Consciousness. | Spirituality.
Classification: LCC BL629.5.A82 J44 2020 (print) | LCC BL629.5.A82
    (ebook) | DDC 204.4--dc23

Published by Larson Publications
4936 NYS Route 414
Burdett, New York 14818 USA
https://www.larsonpublications.com

30 29 28 27 26 25 24 23 22 21 20
10 9 8 7 6 5 4 3 2

Disclaimer: The teachings presented in this book are not a substitute for qualified medical, psychological, or psychiatric diagnosis and treatment. They are meant as a pointer to the essential nature that underlies all conditions.

Dedication

For all beings everywhere, seeking the truth of love.

Contents

open, you will die as the 'you' you think you are and be reborn into awakeness. And even if you are alive as this awakeness for one moment, the revolution has begun. It is the end of the war of inner conflict. And the beginning of silence as the true song of your life."

"Love is a force that moves in us as natural intelligence, the kind of intelligence that takes care of the whole not just the individual parts. It takes care of the whole body, the whole human being, the whole society, the whole nation, the whole world."

"The whole purpose of my teaching is to ignite your own inner authority, to help see where you give yourself away, to show how your own need for love or recognition or acceptance is keeping you small. And to invite you to stand as openness in the face of all the world throws at you."

Acknowledgments

The mystery of life weaves many threads—mostly invisible—to bring us to right where we are. Some of the more visible threads that led to the writing and publication of this book, I give thanks for here. Specifically, Paula Jacobs—sincere seeker of truth, enthusiastic advocate for my work, and friend—who planted the seed of my teaching in upstate New York and introduced me to the wonderful Wisdom's Goldenrod Center. Through my connection with them I was led to Paul Cash (a.k.a. Randy) and Amy Opperman Cash—who together make up Larson Publications—and to whom my gratitude extends for their vision and compassionate guidance in bringing this book into the world. I also give thanks to Andrew Holmes for carrying the torch of possibility by pursuing an unknown path in support of my work.

Closer to home, my husband and beloved Kavi Jezzie Hockaday has been instrumental in igniting the original idea for this book, lovingly giving his attention to the task of collating and editing the transcripts that created its foundation, and gently holding the space for me to dive in to the writing process.

And, of course, this book would not exist without the countless people who have brought their innermost questions to my meetings and retreats over the years. It is through these intimate dialogues that I have been informed of the urgency to close the gap between spirituality and the human experience.

The Invitation of Openness

"I invite you to reject nothing, welcome everything, and surrender into the deepest falling of the open heart."

Over the years of dialoging with spiritual seekers—listening to stories of challenges and confusions on the path of awakening, listening to questions about how to attain the holy grail of enlightenment, or how to transcend the world and its suffering, or how to hold onto peace once it has been glimpsed—I have come to see that underneath all the seeming convolutions of the spiritual journey is just one issue: the refusal to meet life without resistance. And so, through the years, my teaching has been refined to its essential message: the invitation to fall into openness. Falling into openness—a dissolution of the psychological knot of ego—is the doorway to freedom.

Initially, my dialogues with seekers tended to revolve around personal concerns—how to find peace in the midst of turbulent emotions, how to deal with the conflict between the demands of everyday life and the inner journey, how to face the fear of aloneness when an intimate relationship ends, and so on. Today, the dialogues inevitably include concerns about the world—how to deal with anxiety about a world in crisis, how to cope with the seemingly endless suffering of sentient beings, whether a collective awakening can save humanity, and so on. So while I mostly speak about the falling away of an inner world—the collapse of psychological structures that uphold a self-identity based on inherited beliefs—I also speak about the collapse of an outer world.

On a personal level, this may be experienced as the falling away of the motivation to chase previously cherished desires and dreams, or the departure of a partner or family member who is threatened by our spiritual journey, or the loss of a job that is no longer meaningful. On a global level, this collapse is experienced as the increasing turbulence of world events, political and economic structures that no longer support us in feeling safe, chaotic weather patterns that threaten life on earth, and a general uncertainty about our future as a species.

While the invitation of openness is a timeless one—it is the essential pointer to freedom that cuts through all cultures, all ages, and all traditions—it is also a very timely one. As collective consciousness exhibits an increasing polarization leading to increased fear of those with a different worldview, it also mirrors the underlying grip of egoic consciousness that fears its own demise. Nations go to war with each other; the ego goes to war with the present moment. The resolution to both the inner tension of ego-self and the outer tension of the world is the willingness to surrender the argument with what is: to meet reality without resistance. This willingness to surrender is a falling—moment to moment—into silent awareness. And it is up to each one of us to take responsibility for this.

Silent awareness is an undivided state in which the dream of separation comes to an end. It is a falling open into our essential nature—a falling into the infinite silence of consciousness that is here prior to the birth of any inner or outer worlds. It is only when we act from this inner silence that there can be right action in the world. But first we must be willing to lose our world.

The world—inner and outer—is always falling apart. When we get right up close and intimate with our experience, we see that every thought is like a drop of rain falling into the ocean, every feeling is like a brush-stroke that fades in the sunlight, every breath is a fleeting whisper. Just like a flower bursting into the glory of a temporary bloom, so our individual lives are a temporal blossoming. Perhaps humanity in its current manifestation is also one flower amongst many, destined to be a blip in cosmic time, blossoming and then dying to make way for the next flower. Without grasping for certainty or meaning or hope, we can meet life without trying to save it and come to rest in something much deeper than the vicissitudes of the world.

It is only when we meet life from the unknown—and that is what silence really is, an open-ended unknownness—that we can really listen to what is true. And only the truth will set us free.

Like most people, I used to meet life with fear. However seemingly loved I was in my relationships or however seemingly successful I was in my academic career, I carried a gaping hole of emptiness like a hungry ghost that demanded to be filled with something. This "something" was sometimes food or pretty dresses, and at other times it was the accumulation of knowledge (initially scientific knowledge and later on spiritual knowledge) or the sense of hope that came from reading self-help books. Of course, none of that alleviated the inner discomfort and eventually it became so unbearable that I wanted to die. I believed it was a physical death that would solve the problem of my human existence, and I attempted suicide several times.

It took me many years to acknowledge that the cause of my pain was the unloved feelings I had buried under a mountain of denial. Rage, shame, hurt, grief . . . they were all knocking on the door of my heart but for a long time I refused to listen, preferring to take refuge in the ivory tower of my mind. Eventually the dam had to break and my perfectly constructed inner (and outer) world fell apart. It was the beginning of a long journey of unravelling identity, welcoming all feelings, and opening to the aliveness of the present moment.

Many years later, on one ordinary day, an existential void—an unfathomable aloneness—arose from deep within and filled me with an overwhelming terror. By grace or by luck—or perhaps it was all the previous years of dancing on the edges of surrender—I didn't do what I usually did when faced with an unbearable feeling of abandonment or powerlessness. I didn't employ any mental acrobatics to avoid the impending sense of doom. I didn't clamber for a way out: I simply stayed exactly where I was. In that instant of my mind standing still, I felt myself reduced to an infinitesimal pin-prick in the vastness of existence. And right there—in the midst of the abject horror of an inevitable annihilation of my self (the "me" I thought myself to be)—I vanished into an eternal nothing-ness. Unexpectedly, this emptiness revealed itself to be the same as an alive fullness, and when I regained my senses in the next instant, I found that all resistance had fallen away—I had fallen into the infinite openness of this moment. It was the end of "my life" and the beginning of life as it is. Just this. Life as itself.

From that moment on, there has been an inner silence—an openness that meets both sky and clouds equally and allows a deep listening to what is essential. This deep listening is available to you, too, in the midst of your ordinary life—whatever your circumstances and wherever you are on your personal journey of spiritual unfoldment. It is available when you meet this moment with curiosity instead of conclusion, when you welcome your feelings into the softness of your heart, and when you slow down enough to allow silent awareness to reveal itself to you.

The dissolution of the tight knot of ego doesn't necessarily happen in one fell swoop. It is more likely to be a gradual process of unfoldment—a weaving in and out of the open spaciousness of being and an often indiscernible erosion of resistance to what is. Your journey of awakening is unique and is unlikely to look like mine—there is no path but the path *you* are walking. But wherever you are on this path and whatever your circumstances, in every moment the freedom of openness is available. And the personal and global crises we experience in today's world offer a potent opportunity to turn our allegiance from the war with reality to the silent awareness that is always here.

I invite you to fall open, even when your world is falling apart.

The pages that follow offer what has become my "essential teaching." It is not a teaching based on knowledge or belief or spiritual tradition, and it is not meant to be read by the mind that wants information. It is based on some of the living dialogues with those who have been drawn to attend my meetings and retreats. As such, I hope to preserve the aliveness of the dialogue by mostly keeping to a question & answer format and providing a context for your own inquiry.

You may find there is much repetition and even contradiction. I invite you to put aside your linear mind, the mind that wants to "get the truth." This book is a transmission. Do not read it. Feel it. It is like the finger pointing to the moon: if you get hung up on the words and concepts, you will only see the finger. You will miss it. But if you look beyond the words, if you feel into what is essential, you will be guided back to the listening in the depth of your heart.

ONE

Falling Apart or Falling Open?

"I'm not interested in how spiritual you are. I'm interested in how willing you are to stand as openness in the face of brokenness and loss."

The Essence of Openness

Openness is your essential nature. It is what was *already here* before the story of your life got created. And it is what remains when the story of your life ends. It is the space within which your experience appears, and disappears. It is the space within which *you* appear and disappear. It is what is *always here*, come heaven or hell. You cannot get rid of it, you cannot taint it or harm it, you can neither add to it nor take away from it. It has no boundary, no edge, no beginning, and no end. It has no substance, no weight, no position, and no conclusion.

Openness is simply itself. It is not a valve that opens and closes. It is not a sea-anemone that expands and retracts. It is not a faucet you turn on and then turn off. It is simply here, as presence itself. Openness underlies the whole of your existence—like the paper on which history is written, like the sky in which the universe hangs, like the emptiness that contains fullness.

Openness is the "I" that sees, that senses, that knows its own experience. And yet it is not experience itself. It is the awareness that recognizes itself. And yet is not identified by itself. It is the consciousness that is *always here*, come what may. And yet this openness is so often missed, so often overlooked and unrecognized. It's as if we look in the other direction, concentrating on the content of our experience, focused on the endless narratives that rise and fall like waves on the surface of the ocean. We are so concerned with finding our identity in our "doing" and "having," in our feeling and thinking, that we get ourselves snarled up in the world of vicissitudes.

There's a fear that if we open, we'll be taken advantage of, we'll be abused or harmed. There's a tendency to believe it's dangerous to be vulnerable or tender—that we'll be overwhelmed by the depth of our feelings, that it will kill us to allow our hearts to be pierced by the horrors of the world. So we employ some clever acrobatics to bypass our experience—to numb out, to stay asleep. These clever strategies are short-term medicine, but don't work in the long run. Eventually we get so contorted, and the internal pressure of keeping ourselves together builds up to such an extent, that we fear we might burst and collapse into a worthless heap of jelly. The fear of falling open is so huge that we refuse to let go of our need to control and resist that which is uncomfortable and unwelcome—what a problem life is, from this perspective!

My invitation is for you to know the unshakeable openness of your essential nature. You can still have healthy boundaries, you can still say *no* when someone is out to harm or hurt you, you can still walk away from abuse, you can still be human and know where you start and where you end in the world of form. It is, of course, necessary to have healthy boundaries on a physical and psychological level in order to navigate the earthly world.

But none of this has anything to do with the openness that is your essential nature—that which is here prior to your *yes* and your *no*, that which is beyond where you start and where you end. Your essential nature—what you truly are beneath the surface appearance of a personality—is infinite and ever-present. When you know this openness as your foundation, then even your most vociferous *no* will not come from reactivity—it will come from love. It will be right action. It will be intelligent response.

The invitation of openness is to fall into the infinity of your true nature. It is from here that true freedom can begin.

"What is freedom?"

When we speak of freedom, there are all sort of ideas as to what this means. The mind imagines freedom to be *"doing what I want, whenever I want,"* never feeling uncomfortable feelings, never feeling pain or sadness or confusion or doubt. The mind imagines freedom to be a kind of super-state of elevated consciousness in which *"I am all-powerful, all-seeing, all-knowing"* and not subject to the human condition of feelings and emotions and the complexities and concerns of living in three-dimensional reality. This kind of freedom is an imagination. The only true freedom is the freedom of openness.

When we live as openness, we live awake—because it's our natural state. It's not an elevated state, it's not a special state, it's not even a spiritual state. It's more essential than that. Essentially, openness is the willingness, the tenacity, the capacity, to meet reality *as it is*. It's the end of resistance. It's the end of resistance to your experience, the end of resistance to your *human* experience.

The human experience inevitably includes loss. It inevitably includes pain. And it inevitably includes heartbreak. The end of resistance means that we can meet all of that, and there is grace in it. It's a grace that includes it all—the whole bloody mess of

being human and the excruciating inevitability of life's movement. There is grace in it because life flows like a river through
you—*as your experience*—and there's no resistance to that. Life
becomes graceful. This is the only true freedom there is—the
freedom to experience the river of grace that is always *here*, in
heaven and in hell.

"Are you saying that I don't need to be spiritual in order to be free?"

I'm saying that there is something more important, more essential, and more direct, than trying to be spiritual.

First of all, develop the art of listening—listen to the narratives that are running the movie of your life. These narratives
are an indicator of how much argument there is with reality.
First of all, you have to see this argument, you have to see how
it plays itself out in the background. It's like the movie director,
and you—and all the parts of you—are the actors on the stage.
Freedom demands that you're honest with yourself about these
narratives, that you develop the capacity for true listening, that
you expose the truth of the narratives running your show.

When you admit that you're giving your allegiance to the
argument with reality, then something starts to crack open. If
you cannot even admit to the argument—if you're attempting
spiritual practice while the argument is still raging in the rest of
your life experience—there's no transformation. The argument
has to come to an end. And then you won't be concerned about
being spiritual or not. Being spiritual won't have any meaning
to it. It's just a phrase, a concept, an idea that cushions us from
the full depth and breadth of our human experience.

When life is met fully open and fully awake, then—and only
then—can there be freedom. It's a freedom that has nothing to
do with an elevated transcendent state. It may have moments
of transcendence, it may weave in and out of both transcendent

and terrestrial states, but all states come and go. The only true lasting state is openness. And openness is what many of us fear the most—because we are seemingly vulnerable in a state of openness. Most likely we've been open in the past and been hurt, so here is the proof that being open is dangerous. Perhaps when you were a child, small and powerless, you were abused. And that powerlessness has become equated with openness and now you're afraid of being open. You're afraid that somebody will take advantage of you, that somebody will tread all over you, that somebody will use you, that somebody will reject you or abandon you. You're afraid that you are so open that you can't function in the world. So it's a good starting point to become sensitive to where you hold back, where you create a subtle tightening around openness, and to be honest about this even if it exposes a feeling of vulnerability.

The beauty, and the paradox, is that openness is where our true strength is. This is where our true power is, where our true invincibility is. Because as openness, there's nothing that can be taken away from you, there's nothing that can be diminished. As openness you are life itself. The fact is, you are not separate from life. To the mind rooted in separation, it might seem as if you're outside of life trying to get something from life or trying to push life away. But the essential truth is that you *are* life. There is no actual separation, except in your imagination. So what harm can truly be done? The physical organism experiences pain—the pain of illness, the pain of loss, the pain of failure, the pain of death. But all these things are inevitable and they only have to do with the form, not with the essential openness that you are.

"My deepest longing is to be free, but the search
for freedom seems to be endless. When will it
stop? When will my search come to fruition?"

Initially, we look for a spiritual teacher or a spiritual teaching or a spiritual practice that will erase all our suffering, that will erase our unwanted feelings and give us what we want. What we want—even if we are not fully conscious of this wanting—is the bliss, the endless peace, the unbounded awareness that we've heard about, or read about, or been promised. What we want is to transcend the messy human experience. When the imaginary reward is not given, we make *this* teacher or *this* teaching or *that* practice "wrong" and we go off to find the "right" teacher or teaching or practice. But the imaginary holy grail never materializes. The search for freedom becomes a kind of battle, with either victory or defeat as the projected outcome.

When the battle exhausts us, when we seek and fail to find what we think we're looking for—when we seek and fail, seek and fail, and seek and fail some more—we arrive at a bifurcation point. The choice here is to collapse into the story of "poor me" or to rise up into awareness. The choice here is to sulk into closure or surrender into openness—to regress, or to evolve. This is your moment of truth! Now that you have failed enough, been broken enough, been worn down enough, been humbled enough, now that you've been stripped of your imaginings of what freedom feels like, now that you have no fantasy to cling to as a lifeline, no holy grail to chase, no idea of what being spiritual means . . . well, now perhaps you can return to rest in the bare facts of what is here. Perhaps now it can stop being a spiritual issue and start being a human issue. The issue is how to be with the bare bones of our human experience. How to stop running away, and just *be here*?!

If you are honest enough with yourself, if you can lay bare to yourself what stands in the way of just being here with what is, you return to yourself. This is not a regression into unconsciousness but a transformation into love. When there is no more attempt to avoid or escape any feeling or experience, you discover there is nothing to run away from and nothing to run toward. You discover that truth is not a perfect state of understanding, nor is it a perfect state of non-feeling. It is the very aliveness of this moment, however it shows up. And this acceptance of what is here, this intimacy with what is here, is the very freedom that you seek.

Now instead of a spiritual high there is a spiritual maturity. You stop rejecting and sulking, and start opening and welcoming. In openness, there is no problem because there is no resistance to what is. The whole spectrum of the human experience—from heaven to hell—is deeply accepted. You stop trying to be spiritual, stop handing over authority to your imaginings of how it should be, and come to rest in the true authority of your innermost openness.

And when you seem to fall, when you seem to fail, when you find yourself back down on your knees broken open by life's vicissitudes, you will remember that you don't need to cower in shame, or fix yourself, or look for salvation in spirituality. You will remember to be right here, in the bare bones of our humanity —in love with the openness that holds every experience.

Is It OK to Fall Apart?

"My world is falling apart, nothing makes sense any more. I feel as if I'm falling apart, I can't keep my life together. I'm afraid. What should I do?"

It really *is* ok to let go, to fall apart. I do not say this lightly, as I have walked this path and understand that fear.

Falling apart sounds scary, so we do everything in our power not to fall apart. We keep our emotions in check, we keep our feelings hidden . . . even from ourselves. We contort ourselves around family rules: they tell us not to rock the boat, not to be too wild, to just fit in with their expectations and everything will be fine. We conform to society's norms: they tell us to work hard, to save for a rainy day, to have a family, to secure our future in order to live a good life. We perform mental acrobatics to convince ourselves that we are fulfilled. We sacrifice our inner truth in order to belong. It seems we will do anything in order to not fall apart, because falling apart conjures up images of devastation, of depression, of despair. And even worse, it conjures up images of a big black void that swallows us up so that there's nothing left of us. It stirs up an existential terror, in which there is no ground beneath us and we are falling into an eternity of emptiness.

But what if the effort of holding it all together becomes just too much? What if you're so weighed down, so constricted, so suffocated by your trying to keep it together, that one day a tiny chink in your armor lets a sliver of light in? And even though it's terrifying, some distant part of you celebrates. Yes, celebrates! Because finally, you can let go. Finally, you can stop trying to hold it all together. But . . . it's so scary. You fear you will die. You fear it is the end of you. So you waver between gripping on for dear life and relishing the letting go. You teeter and totter, neither this way nor that, stuck in resistance to the inevitable. But when the cracks appear and a great fear arises, it's a potent invitation to let go—a sign that an old world is dying and a new one is being born. It's a sign that a more true *you* is ready to emerge, like the butterfly releasing itself from the chrysalis.

So, it really *is* ok to let go—to fall apart. In fact, you have no choice because eventually you will be forced to let it all go—when you take that final breath before you leave this earthly body. You might as well do it now—you might as well experiment and see what happens when you give yourself permission to fall apart.

Perhaps you'll discover that falling apart is not what it seemed in your imaginings. You might discover that what falls apart is the arsenal of defenses you've been building up to protect you from heartbreak and grief and hurt and loss. You might discover that what falls apart is your idea of being separate from the fullness of life's flow, from the wild grace of the earthly experience, from the holy brokenness of this crazy ride of being human. And you just might discover that everything you imagined held you together has no real validity.

You might just discover what really holds you together is the breath that weaves you into existence. You might just discover that in falling apart you are resurrected into this sacred moment. You might just discover that you are held in the open hand of being-ness.

So yes, it's ok to fall apart. It's your feelings you're scared of—your vulnerability, your shame, your brokenness, your helplessness. But feelings cannot extinguish who you really are. Once the tempest has moved through you, you are left clean and naked, stripped of the burden of pretending to be who you are not. And in this naked awareness, you see that you're not really falling apart—you are falling open.

"The idea of falling is still very scary to me.
Can you say more about that?"

I speak a lot about falling—falling into openness, falling into the unknown. To the mind these words are scary, they don't make sense. But even though the mind scrambles to understand and comes up with all sorts of theories as to what this means, there's something in each of us to which it speaks so deeply, with which it resonates so deeply. Because this falling into openness is our deepest longing.

This openness *is* the freedom that we're seeking. It's the freedom from our own mental narratives—freedom from the clenched fist in the belly, freedom from the armoring around the heart, freedom from the defended-ness of the personali-ty-self. This freedom is what we're really seeking through every-thing we're doing, whether it be in the outer world of acquiring wealth or security or relationship or the inner world of positive thoughts and good feelings. This freedom from our mental tight-ness brings an openness that allows us to relax—although this relaxation is mostly temporary.

We yearn to know the freedom of this openness. We yearn for it because it is our true nature. It is where we came from, it is where we're going, and it is what we already are. So when I speak about falling, when I speak about openness, I speak directly to that longing. This speaking is not a language of the ordinary world because it's not relevant there. We have to function in and navigate the world, so a different focus of language is used for that. But when we embark on the path of deep inner inquiry—when we gather in a *sangha* (spiritually oriented group) or go on spiritual retreat, we need a language to help us tap into this new freedom. We can receive nourishment just from the dialoguing itself, just from the language itself, just from the places it takes us. There is a deep nourishment in that.

So, even though the mind cannot understand this openness, how can we recognize it . . . more and more? How can we give our allegiance to this . . . more and more? Even when there are hardships in life, even when there are unwelcome experiences? Even when there is pain and loss and brokenness? These are the questions. And by asking the questions, there is a discovery.

This discovery has nothing to do with the mind's knowledge. The discovery happens as we soften. It happens as we start to trust ourselves, trust ourselves in listening more deeply, in speaking more deeply, questioning more deeply. Then it starts to happen by itself. It comes as an inner intelligence, an intelligence that takes us all the way home to the open hand waiting for us at the core of our being.

Living as the Open Hand

"The metaphor of the open hand is very resonant. It speaks to my innermost. But how do I live as the open hand?"

Well, it has nothing to do with how awake or enlightened you are. It has nothing to do with how spiritual you are. Nor has it anything to do with how kind or compassionate or charitable or good you are. Although all these qualities will start to start to come through you when you know your true nature as openness, and when you live from that openness naturally.

Living as the open hand means softening, letting go, and relaxing within the experience that you are having—*whatever* that experience is. This softening is neither spiritual nor unspiritual. It is neither enlightened nor unenlightened. Whatever experience is happening within you—whether it is heaven or it is hell—is a potent invitation to the infinite openness of love. You are invited to notice where the clenched fist is still operating, where there is turning away, or numbing out, or the tug of wanting something to be different than how it is. Even if the wanting it to be different is here as your experience, you are invited to relax into that. It can get very subtle. And you can get so much closer to your innermost. What I'm really speaking about here, is the deepest acceptance of your inner experience—because your experience is all you can know. In the deepest acceptance, you meet reality *as it is*. This deep acceptance is what it takes to live fully awake.

In this deep acceptance, you meet reality as the open *yes*. It doesn't mean that you necessarily like it. It doesn't mean that it goes away. It doesn't mean that you don't feel discomfort. It doesn't mean that you wake up and see it all as an illusion and it doesn't hurt anymore. It means that you bow down to what is. And what *is* includes fear—both the fear of meeting unwelcome feelings and the deeper existential fear of falling into an unknown dimension of openness.

So how do you meet reality as the open hand of *yes* when the clenched fist of resistance is still fighting for supremacy?

There's a way of seeing more clearly the mechanism of resistance: whenever you feel discomfort, whenever you feel you've fallen off the enlightened heights of peace and grace and transcendence, whenever you feel that there is something wrong and you shouldn't be feeling like this, you can be sure that you have created yourself as unworthy. There's a question in this that can open the door to a deeper insight: unworthy in the eyes of whom? If you look closely—and even more and more closely than that—the reply is: unworthy in the eyes of your own imagination. The fact of the matter is, there's no-one "out there" judging you, telling you that you're not good enough or perfect enough or spiritual enough. These are all narratives in your restless mind—the voices of your parents or your schoolteachers or your religious leaders. And even if there is someone in your close environment seemingly telling you that you are wrong, you have internalized that voice and imagine it to have a greater authority than your own. If you look into your innermost—into the space which is closer than any narrative—you will discover none of these "external authorities" are actually here now, in *this* moment.

So whenever you feel not good enough, not enlightened enough, or that something is wrong in your experience, that's the clue that you're fighting your inner experience, that you are divided within your own experience. This is the terror of the inner war. When you become sensitive to this inner division, this is exactly the right time for transformation. This is the right time to relax, to say "Yes, this is *here* . . . it is *as it is.*" This is the right time to be willing to stand as openness in the midst of pain, in the midst of loss, in the midst of discomfort. This is the right time to stand as openness in the face of that which you don't want and that which you don't like.

It is up to you. No one can teach you this, or wave a magic wand to make it happen. It is up to you to search within and ask yourself if you are willing to bow down to what is.

Trust on the Spiritual Path

"Is it important to have a sense of trust on
the spiritual path?"

First of all, we should examine: what are we putting our trust in? If we look carefully, we will see that trust implies "hope in the future." In other words, we hope that things will turn out in our favor. We hope that if we have a certain attitude or a certain belief or a certain understanding, we will be taken care of by a higher power. We hope that if we trust in our own positive thoughts, no harm will ever come to us. We hope that if we diligently follow a certain spiritual practice, we will achieve everlasting peace and happiness. We hope that trust will save us from an uncertain world and from a broken heart.

But trust in *something* is a false safety net. It may satisfy the

mind, but it does not satisfy the being—because it is a postpone-
ment of the fullness that is already *here*. Why are you waiting
for a better tomorrow? Why are you waiting to find fulfillment
when you will have achieved something or acquired something
or understood something? What if the future doesn't unfold the
way you hope it will? What then happens to the trust you once
had—will it be broken? And will you ever be able to trust again?
As long as trust is based on the hope of better future, you are a
million miles from the gift of life that's already here.

Be courageous enough to meet life from the unknown—without a safety net, without hope, without past, and without future.
Without the hope of salvation—without running away from or
running toward anything in your mind—you are forced to fall
into the open space of being-ness. And in this openness, you
fall out of time and out of imagination, right into the present. In
other words, you become present—you become totally available
to the essential being-ness of life.

In presence, you and life have collapsed into each other—
there is no longer a "future life," it's all happening *now*. In this
eternal now, you and life are one—and when you are one with
what *is*, how can you possibly fear what *is*? It's like fearing your
self, and that's ridiculous—because your self, the being-ness that
you already are, never leaves you. Being-ness is totally depend-
able—it is always *here*.

Now you are in touch with a deeper kind of trust—one that
is not based on *something*. It is no longer a conceptual trust, but
one that is inherent in the nature of presence. It is inherent in the
nature of life, because life is always what is here in the present—it
can't be anywhere else. This deeper trust has no meaning to the
mind, but complete meaningfulness to your natural state. And
even if you fail, even if life leads you to a seeming dead-end,
even if you are handed an unwanted circumstance, even if you

don't get to your desired destination of perfect happiness, even if your heart is broken open over and over again—you will still trust the presence that holds it all.

Openness and Boundaries

"What about personal boundaries? Doesn't openness mean I have to always say yes? And isn't that dangerous? How do I protect myself from harm if I'm open all the time? And how can I learn to be open if I have a history of trauma and abuse?"

The openness I speak of has nothing to do with your personal history. It has nothing to do with whether you've been abused or hurt. It has nothing to do with self-protection or personal boundaries.

The openness I speak of is beyond all that. It is beneath all that. It is more ever-present than all that. The openness I speak of has no opposite, it cannot close. It is the space within which you—and the story of your life—appear and disappear. It is the open awareness that holds it all. It is awareness itself. This awareness is always here, it cannot come and go. It can either be recognized and free you from fear, or remain unrecognized and let you remain enslaved to the false authority of ego's narratives—and that is up to you.

Is it safe to say *yes?* Even though you feel shaky, you feel vulnerable, you feel raw and tender, you feel unsafe because you learned that saying *yes* could hurt? Yes, it is safe to say *yes,* when you feel a *yes* in your belly—even though the mind may be tainted by a bad memory. Is it safe to say *no?* Even though you learned that saying *no* got you into trouble, and now you feel bad about yourself when you say *no,* as if you've transgressed a boundary and will be punished? Yes, it is safe to say *no*, when you feel a *no* in your belly—even though the heart trembles.

You see, saying *yes* and saying *no* is your birthright as a human being. Wholesome personal boundaries are a necessity in a world of seven billion individuals. There's a sword of personal truth that must be wielded as you navigate this earthly dimension. Without this you are subject to the unconsciousness of others and you are subject to the vicissitudes of the world.

And yet, the openness of your essential nature as awareness underpins it all and is untouched by your *yes* and your *no*. This open awareness is the foundation of you and from this place arises right action—sometimes it is a *yes*, sometimes it is a *no*, both arise out of the open sky of awareness.

You are—and always were—that open awareness. All you have to do is recognize that.

"But don't I have to heal from trauma before I can awaken?

The question of trauma surfs on the edge of psychological inquiry and spiritual inquiry.

Certainly, by working sensitively and intelligently with deeply held stress in the nervous system we can support the unravelling of physical, emotional, and mental contractions that are so often obstacles to true awakening. But focusing on the one who cannot be fully present because of what happened in the past can easily reify the idea of a separate self that suffers.

It's a delicate dance between holding the story of trauma in the tenderness of open heart and stepping off the merry-go-round of "me and my story." At some point, when the examination of what went wrong has exhausted itself, the free-fall into the abyss of being is more inviting than holding on to any identity as victim. But this time must come naturally, it cannot be forced. There must be a natural evolution in which the self becomes "sick and tired" of itself and the only way out of suffering is to irrevocably and irreversibly surrender to what is here.

The question of trauma does a balancing act between self as the "center of life" and "life without a center" when we awaken out of self-centeredness. Right here, dancing lightly on this edge, we are invited to recognize that nothing can prevent us from fully experiencing the fullness of this moment . . . other than the thought *"I can't."* We are invited to recognize that nothing is actually repeated, that every experience is a fresh one appearing in this present moment, that reality is only *now.*

In some ways we have all been subject to trauma—we all have trigger-points which cause us to defend, attack, numb out, and so on in order to protect ourselves from being hurt, from experiencing the trauma of feeling unloved, rejected, abandoned, unseen. Many of us come from broken homes, dysfunctional families, traumatized ancestry. We live in traumatic times of an exponentially increased pace of life and the looming threat of global annihilation. The very fact of our human existence is a trauma to the soul as it incarnates to experience itself as an individuated form. Believing ourselves to be separate from our origin of wholeness, we often spend a lifetime seeking a return to that sense of oneness—either consciously through spiritual practice or unconsciously through seeking gratification in pleasure and possessions. This trauma comes to an end when we realize that the identification with form is a dream . . . and we never actually left home.

Right here, in the realization of this unending presence, we can finally rest. Trauma needs to be held, to know that it finally can come home to its original nature as wholeness. The goal isn't seeking a resolution to its problem of reactivity, it's not seeking to inhabit a person with improved self-esteem, it's not seeking to mend that which is broken. It's seeking to know the unbroken amidst the mess of being human.

It's not that your life suddenly becomes perfect—it's that you finally can stand as openness in the midst of imperfection. Whether that imperfection is to do with your personal circumstances or whether it's to do with the imperfection of the world, it's all the same. When you truly know yourself as the open awareness which cannot be born and cannot die, then all of it becomes exquisite.

As this open awareness, you are fully present—there's no compulsion to run away from this moment exactly as it is. The world is no longer a problem to you. Your life is no longer a problem to you. *You* are no longer a problem to you. This doesn't mean that you're elevated above the imperfection. It means you're right *here* where you are.

Right here, in this forever unfolding moment, the unbroken presence can hold it all. And in this holding, everything comes home to love.

TWO

Welcoming Everything Home

"What is broken is the doorway to gold. What is shattered is the entrance to inconceivable love. What brings you to your knees is not a punishment but God's invitation. Your brokenness is holy."

The Beloved Is Inside Every Experience

St. John of the Cross said, "Take my lofty spiritual concepts and plunge them into darkness and then burn them. Let me love only you Beloved. Let me, quietly and with unutterable simplicity, only love you."[1] These potent words point to the futility of holding onto the idea that understanding the "absolute truth" will enable us to rise above our human experience and achieve a higher state of consciousness that's more desirable or worthy. They point to the revelation that transcendence is a denial of the Beloved that is ever-present in the naked fact of our humanity.

The Beloved *is* the open hand of love. This love has no beginning and no end. It is not contained. It is not conditional. It is simply the deepest acceptance of what is here. This stops the human experience being one of the *me* trying to get something from life in order to make *me* happy or successful or safe. It stops the human experience being about trying to fight life or push away life so that I can stay in my comfort zone. It stops the belief that life is happening to *me* . . . either according to my wishes, my expectations, my dreams, and my hopes or according to my fears, my nightmares, and my suffering. The deepest acceptance of what is here—the utter simplicity of loving what is—puts an end to resistance. No longer is there a tight fist. No longer is there a push and pull. No longer is there a *me* and *life*.

The truth is I and life are one. It's a mystical union of self and existence.

"What does welcoming everything mean?"

Welcoming everything means tenderness, kindness, acceptance. In other words, non-resistance to whatever you're experiencing. I'm not talking about circumstances—such as when somebody smacks you in the mouth and you move to defend yourself, or you're in an abusive relationship and you leave to protect yourself, and so on. I'm talking about your energetic experience—the internal landscape of feelings and sensations, the *"felt-sense"* of this very moment.

It's a delicate situation though, as it's easy to take on this felt-sense as an identity—a way of making yourself wrong about your feelings because you're not strong or spiritual or enlightened. But don't turn your feelings into another battleground, don't let these feelings be a reason for more conflict or argument. Simply allow yourself to *feel* what is here—especially if this feeling has been previously denied.

Your tenderness, your kindness, your acceptance—your *welcoming*-ness—is the doorway through which everything that has been previously unloved can "come home" and return to source. Just feeling the energy, allowing it, letting it be . . . and what was a tight contraction is able to relax. Perhaps not all at once—more likely this relaxation happens in small increments. It's like a small child or a scared animal—as the energy of contraction starts to feel held more and more, it starts to feel safe more and more, and starts to relax more and more.

What is this energy—this "felt-sense"—held by? It's held by openness itself. In this openness, it stops being a monster and you stop resisting your feelings. It's as if an outdated psychological mechanism of defense and attack unravels itself—something melts in you, something softens in you, something deeply relaxes. Over time, the seemingly terrible feeling that you avoided for so long stops knocking on the door because it already has come in and dissolved into the Beloved.

Only *you*—I keep saying this—only *you* can do this. No external power can make it happen for you. It's not a "doing" from the egoic self, it's not about applying brute force and determination. But neither is it an abdication of responsibility, a kind of "spiritual laziness." It's a willingness to welcome everything—to be vigilant, to be courageous, to be in humility toward what is here in your experience. This willingness must arise from the depth of you—because you really have had enough of the inner argument with what is. There's no waiting for grace to do this for you. Only *you* can turn toward this willingness in each moment . . . now, and now, and *now*.

"Does this mean that loving every-thing puts an end to fear?"

Yes. Love puts an end to fear. You no longer fear your experience because it's not outside of you, it's not something that happens *to* you. It's no longer that which torments you. It is simply love in disguise. It is love in disguise because it offers you the invitation to open within that experience. You come to see that every experience contains an invisible hand of openness that always extends itself to you. This openness is the ultimate fulfillment. It's what you are really looking for, but so often miss.

It is here both in the experience of getting what you want *and* in the experience of not getting what you want. In the experience of getting what you want—you find a lover and you feel loved, you get married and feel secure, you get the qualification or the job you want and you feel recognized, you give birth to a child and feel complete—there is a subtle grip of *"I got it"* and *"I don't want to lose it."* You start to wrap yourself around the object that promises eternal fulfillment. Fear comes in because you don't want to lose what you have . . . and you miss the invitation of openness.

In the experience of not getting what you want—your lover leaves you, your marriage falls apart, your career fails, you lose your home or your money or your child or your dog—there is a less subtle grip, the tight fist of *"I don't want this"* or *"This shouldn't be happening,"* and you attempt to reject it or fix it or run away from it. Fear takes over because you can't control life, you don't want to feel the pain of loss . . . and you miss the invitation of openness.

"How should I deal with fear when it shows up?"

The invitation is to become sensitive, to become highly attuned to where this subtle grip takes over, to notice when there is a subtle tightening—either holding on for dear life or pushing life away. In that moment of noticing, you have a choice. It doesn't matter when you notice, as long as there is a moment of noticing. In this moment, you have choice. It's a choice that doesn't come from the mind. It's a choice that comes from the tenderness of the heart. It's a turning away from the circumstances of life, and a turning toward your innermost.

Your innermost is the tenderness of the heart, and here the doorway of surrender opens. It's the surrender of ego-mind's grip on reality . . . and you don't have to do anything. You cannot *do* the surrender. The tenderness of the heart doesn't attempt to do anything with its experience . . . it simply is *with* the experience. It is intimate with the experience, it is close to the experience, and in that intimacy and that closeness, you come closer to yourself. You come closer to your true self, your true self as openness. Your essential nature, in the innermost, *is* openness.

Everything else—every maneuver that doesn't bring you closer to your experience, that doesn't bring you closer to tenderness—is a cover-up. That cover-up is what makes life burdensome, that cover-up is what makes life a struggle, that cover-up is what makes you fearful. So, how to deal with fear? By noticing the places and the moments in your life when you do *not* turn toward tenderness. Don't look for freedom from fear in transcendence, don't look for freedom from fear in some myth of spirituality. Don't run away from fear. Turn toward fear and meet it with tenderness.

Life is your spiritual teacher, the only true teacher there is. Become sensitive to the places and moments where you *don't* turn toward tenderness in your relationships—in your relationship to your spouse or to your children or to your dog, in your relationship to your work or your creativity or to your sense of mission, in your relationship to your bank account and to your taxes. Become sensitive to the places and moments you *don't* turn toward tenderness in your relationship to your body—the aches and pains, the loss of eyesight or motion, the sickness and the wellness.

Every relationship is your teacher. In every relationship, you either operate as the tight fist of resistance and it's a struggle, a burden, a nightmare . . . or you turn toward the tenderness of the heart, become intimate with your experience, and simply love it. This—right *here*—is where the Beloved lives. This is the invitation of openness, the invitation of surrender, the invitation of tenderness—it is right here. Look to your life for the doorway to freedom.

The Power of Tenderness

*"Are you saying that I should meet all
uncomfortable feelings with tenderness?"*

Yes. Everything yearns to come home to your heart. Every energy that exists—everything that appears as your experience—yearns to return to source, to the formless. And your heart is a doorway to the formless.

The unwanted energies, the unwelcome feelings—whether abandonment or rejection or betrayal or grief or failure or vulnerability or fear—are here not to torment you, even though it may appear that way. They are here to invite you to welcome everything.

The invitation is to surrender the tenacious grip of reactivity toward what you're feeling. It's an invitation to surrender the habit of rejecting, denying, pushing away, and telling yourself *"This shouldn't be happening."* This surrender can't be done with the same mind that created the reactivity in the first place. You can get closer to surrender only by being willing for everything to come home to rest in you. It's an act of love . . . an act of kindness, of tenderness.

This love, this tenderness, is not only the deepest longing of your heart, it's also the deepest longing of everything that exists. Every energy and every feeling yearns to come home to die in you. It's not a horrible death, it's a beautiful death. It's a death in which everything that existed as form—the feeling that was tormenting you, the energy that was solidified into your experience—dissolves into formless openness. When you meet trauma or heartbreak or fear with tenderness and it dies in you, it's done . . . it doesn't revisit you.

This doesn't mean you then live in a feelingless place, in an untouchable place, in an elevated or perfect place. But it does mean that the particular energy, in the form it first visited you, no longer exists. So when you experience something again—another energy, another feeling—it will never be a replay of the past. It will be fresh. It will be a new wave. It won't be a repetition. It only seems to be a repetition if you keep rejecting and denying it. If you reject and deny, it will keep knocking at the door again and again . . . and it will have that smell of the past, that heaviness, that leftover feeling. But when a new wave comes—a new heartbreak, a new love, a new rage, a new grief—it won't be a leftover from the past, it won't be carried over. Now it can be met freshly.

Tenderness is the doorway to the depth of your heart. Your willingness to be tender is the only remedy for the willfulness of mind. When surface mind bows down to deep heart, this is the same as mind bowing down to God. Eventually when mind bows down enough, it will take its rightful place—not as the master, but as the servant. Now mind can serve truth, it can serve that which is true in your innermost.

The Indian poet Rabindranath Tagore was right in saying, "To find God, you must welcome everything." In other words, in order to know yourself and everything that exists as Godness—in order to know the essential goodness in yourself and in everything that exists—you must welcome everything into your heart. When we see with the eyes of the heart, there is only one totality, one being, one God. There are not lots of separate beings, some of which are God and some of which are not, some of which are good and some of which are not.

When you meet the reality of your experience with tenderness—over and over again—you may come to realize the essential nature of life as oneness. This oneness is the unbounded openness—the infinite space or consciousness—within which everything appears.

> *"I've been trying to awaken for many years,*
> *but still I don't know how to surrender."*

This question of how to surrender most often comes when the exhaustion of trying to awaken reaches its peak . . . *trying* to do a spiritual practice, *trying* to meditate, *trying* to be mindful, *trying* to open, *trying* to accept.

When trying exhausts itself, the possibility of surrender comes to the forefront. And then the question arises: *"How to surrender?"* But this question comes from the wrong place. It's not a matter of *how* it can be done. There is no formula for the mind . . . the mind cannot do it or understand it. When a circumstance is challenging, when life rocks our world, when there is loss or pain of some kind, surrender becomes impossible because the mind does not want to surrender to a circumstance and to an experience that it really doesn't want.

It's more useful to turn your attention to tenderness. Tenderness is the same as surrender. It's not about having loving thoughts or sending thoughts of compassion toward that which is the cause of your pain and suffering, whether it be another person, a circumstance in your life, or a world event. It's not about using the mind to "practice tenderness" or to "do tenderness." Tenderness is what remains when you stop giving attention to the narratives in your mind. When something happens in your life and you experience a feeling you don't like, the habitual tendency is to wrap a whole bunch of narratives around that experience: *"This shouldn't be happening," "I shouldn't be feeling this," "They shouldn't have done that"* and so on. These narratives create resistance. These narratives create the clenched fist. These narratives create the suffering. When you stop giving attention to the narratives, what remains is a kind of quietness. It's a space, a softness. It's not a weakness, but an openness.

Tenderness is the openness of an inner silence. This silence can't be created by the mind and its attempt to change experience. It can't be created by having positive thoughts. It can't be created by having loving thoughts. Silence has nothing to do with thinking, because whether the mind engages in positive thinking or negative thinking it's still producing a narrative, it's still mounting an attempt to try and fix something.

Tenderness is what remains when there's no attempt to fix anything. I'm not suggesting that you avoid tending to circumstances that require your care and attention. I'm talking about your inner experience in response to circumstances, which is where the suffering is. The suffering is not in *what* happens, but in *how* you respond to what happens.

Surrender doesn't necessarily mean the discomfort goes away. If there is an agenda—an expectation that your suffering comes to an end—then it is not surrender. True surrender means you fall into a deeper place within yourself, irrespective of your feelings. In your depth, there is no division—there is only the deepest acceptance, there is only openness. Openness is the space within which everything happens—and who you are *is* openness. Beneath the divided mind, beneath the mind that spews out narratives, there is only openness. This openness is the tender place within you that simply and utterly meets what is here *as it is*. So, instead of trying to change what's happening on the outside—instead of trying to fix a relationship or trying to fix the world—change your relationship to your inner experience because that's where true change begins.

The simple teaching of tenderness has the power to change everything, from the inside out.

Your Brokenness Is Holy

"What about really dark emotions, like rage and shame and grief?"

First of all, be very honest with yourself. Do you run away from your pain, your shame, your secret rage and private grief? Do you stuff those unwanted feelings into the dark recesses of your belly, cover them over with things to do, things to get, things to eat? Do you turn away from disappointment, rejection, failure, and regret, pretending they don't visit you in the dark of night? Do you try to fix your fractured heart, shut down your restless mind, stick a band-aid over your emotional wounds, to prevent the dirt and mess of being human from oozing out? Do you turn to spirituality as a salve for all that you think is wrong with you, holding tight to the belief that transcendence will prove your perfection once and for all?

Now, listen very closely. Listen—sweetly and gently—to the deepest knowing in you. Listen to that which is deeper than fear, deeper than discomfort, deeper than shame or trauma or loss. Listen to the visitors who knock on your heart—knocking from the inside. Shame, pain, loneliness, grief, and more—all these are your allies not your foes. They yearn to come in, to be acknowledged, to be accepted, to be loved. For—as emphasized earlier—what is broken is the doorway to gold, what is shattered is the entrance to inconceivable love, what brings you to your knees is not a punishment but God's invitation.

The purpose of everything in your experience that seems so unwelcome is to reveal to you—not conceptually as a belief, but experientially as a visceral recognition—that your essential nature is *prior* to all experience. Who you *really* are is prior to all content—whether the content is ecstatic or terrifying, or anything in between. Who you really are is the open awareness—the space or consciousness—that is always here. But you only get closer to this realization when you stop avoiding the content of your experience. The attempt to avoid meeting what scares you, prevents you from this deeper knowing of your true nature. So, when terror arises, when an intense unbearability arises, know that it is God knocking at the door from the inside—it's not the devil trying to torment you. It's not that there's something terribly wrong, but that something immensely good is unfolding . . . it is God's invitation from your innermost.

The question is not *"How can I get rid of dark emotions?"* but *"Am I willing to embrace the grit and grace of being human? Am I willing to reject nothing, welcome everything, and surrender into the deepest falling of the open heart?"*

Listen closely. Hear it inside you: Your brokenness is holy.

"I find shame a particularly difficult emotion to embrace."

Yes, there is often such trying to overcome it, to get rid of shame, to cover it up with bravado and smiles, with cleverness and wit strategically placed to hide the unwanted, the unforgivable.

We wish we were not so scarred, not so tarnished, not so cracked and grimy that we had to bury it deep inside, so that now we are shocked when the monstrous energy of shame knocks on the door at unexpected and inconvenient moments. We wish we had been born more perfect, more lovable, more worthy of attention and acceptance, so that we would not have to contort ourselves into a thousand shapes to convince ourselves we are good enough. Shame sits like a dark stone, heavy and toxic with years of neglect. It's a guilty secret we hold onto, as if letting it fly free would kill us. We'd rather hold tight to the familiarity of sinfulness than fall into the unknown hand of love.

But truly, the only sin you ever encounter is in the move away from your original innocence. Do you think you can enter the kingdom of heaven by walking away from yourself? Do you think you can find yourself in acquisitions or trophies for the mind? Is the grass greener in the pastures of the imagination? Or is it that you cannot not bear your own fullness? And now you yearn to come home to your original nature. You long for rest. You long to be held in the pause between breaths. But somehow that old foe—the immovable shadow of shame—has woven itself into all the spaces, filling you with an awful foreboding.

Here is the way through—welcome shame, like a neglected friend. Open the door, even just a little, when shame comes knocking from the inside. Offer it up to the light of exposure, a sacrament in the fire of acceptance. Let it burn in the openness, let it consume itself in the vulnerability, let it be transformed in the heart of an innocent *yes*.

As you stand here—bearing the unbearable—you may discover that in reality you have never moved away from yourself. You have always been here as this perfect presence. No ghostly thought or belief or feeling can subtract from the fullness of this present moment. You may discover that no experience is ever repeated, but that each one appears as something new in the freshness of now.

And, as you stay right where you are—gloriously and unashamedly open to what is here—you may discover that shame is not a punishment, but a portal to your true power.

The End of Seeking

*"All my seeking has brought me to a kind of
breaking point and I feel I can't go on. I'm still
longing for inner peace, but nothing seems to help.
How can I move beyond this impasse?"*

At some point on the journey of spiritual seeking there comes a bifurcation point, a kind of fork in the road, where the road splits in two directions. You arrive at this bifurcation point when all the spiritual experiences, openings, insights, awakenings, highs, realizations, and understandings still do not satisfy the call to come home, when there is still a deep longing for something more. When this tension builds up, there comes a breaking point. And here you have a choice. I say it's a choice, because it feels as if there's some personal agency at this place. At a deeper level, there is no choice—the road is already taken, it is inevitable that you will walk in this direction and not the other direction. But let's say there's a choice—because it feels as if you're being asked to make a choice, asked to overcome some inertia.

So, at this bifurcation point, there can be a kind of resignation, a collapse, a turning away from listening to the depth in you. You might say to yourself, *"Well, none of it's working anyway, it hasn't brought me lasting peace, it hasn't brought me lasting enlightenment, so I might as well just give up and give in to my reactivity and habitual tendencies."* Or, at this bifurcation point, a new inquiry could be birthed in you. Instead of asking *"How can I reach enlightenment?"* you might ask a different question, one that takes you closer to your human experience not further away from it.

When you ask, *"How can I more deeply and more tenderly embrace my human experience?"* then you make a huge turn-around from looking for a spiritual high to growing foundations for true spiritual maturity. Spiritual maturity does not see a dichotomy between awakeness and humanness. Instead, it is an opening to the whole spectrum of the human experience with all its challenges, all its brokenness, and all its failures. It includes every possible feeling, so that nothing is made an enemy in your mind. There is no more the attempt to fight or reject or suppress or pretend. You meet the whole of the human experience with tender openness.

This tender openness is a big internal shift from looking for an escape from the human experience to being fully being present with what is. It doesn't necessarily always feel the way you want it to feel, but it does mean that feelings are no longer the enemy.

"Are you saying I should give up hoping that
the spiritual search will bring me to peace?"

Hope is a symptom of the psychological desire to escape, to avoid that which we don't like, that which we don't want, that which we're afraid of, that which we deem to be an enemy.

Essentially, what we deem to be an enemy is a feeling we don't like. We don't like to feel fear. We don't like to feel uncertainty. We don't like to feel discomfort. We don't like to feel heartbreak. We don't like to feel grief. We don't like to feel despair. We don't like to feel aloneness. There are a lot of things we don't like to feel. There are a lot of enemies seemingly *out there,* but actually all *in here.*

The spiritual search, the desire to end suffering, is (at least initially) invested with a hidden agenda . . . to avoid feeling anything that we don't like. So off we go, looking for the right teacher, the right teaching, the right spiritual method, the right meditation practice. And all this activity is invested with an agenda, a hope that *that* teacher, *that* teaching, *that* meditation, *that* practice, *that* understanding, *that* knowledge will give us what we want. And what we want is the end of feeling anything that we don't like. If that teacher, that teaching, that method, that understanding doesn't bring us the reward of freedom from pain, then we turn away from it and go off looking for another teacher, another teaching, another method, another understanding. And so the search continues.

We call this the search for truth, but it's really not the truth. If truth is something that someone can give you, if truth is something you can find, then it's really not the truth. As soon as truth is objectified, then it's not the truth. As soon as truth is something we can possess, we have created an imaginary truth out of our own invested agenda, our invested need for safety and comfort. We can search for this truth and maybe we find it but then we lose it. And so the search goes on.

Eventually we get broken enough and beaten enough and humbled enough to come right back to where we are. I don't mean that we regress, but we return more naked. Having gone through a process of seeking and failing, having been stripped of erroneous imaginings of what truth or freedom or awakening look like, we return to the bare fact of what is *here.*

At this point the process stops being a spiritual issue and starts being a human issue. How can we just be with the bare facts, the bare bones of our human experience? If we have been sincere enough, if we have been honest enough with ourselves, if we have been willing to expose to ourselves all the little tricky saboteurs—all the little tricky beliefs that stand in the way of simply being here in the deepest acceptance of what is here in our experience—then we are not likely to return to more seeking. Nor return to more shrinking. If our self-exposure has been ruthlessly honest, we can no longer look for the answer outside of ourselves—in a teacher or teaching or practice or knowledge—in the hope of spiritual salvation.

What can come next is a return to openness—the only place from which deep listening can occur. It is a return to innocence, before we were tainted by fear and hope. It is a return to true aliveness. It means we have no more enemies. There is no longer the attempt to avoid or escape anything—feeling, emotion, or sensation. Here is the peace that we seek. Here is the freedom that we seek. We stop trying to avoid or fix or change the human experience.

This is the end of seeking. I'm speaking primarily here about the seeking based in the escape from suffering. But it is really the end of all seeking—even when the seeking is for more joy or more purpose or more grace. That is still a seeking for more fulfillment, and an avoidance of the true fulfillment that is here when there is no seeking for another "more." That is a more subtle kind of seeking, but still it doesn't bring freedom.

True freedom comes when *all* seeking comes to an end— when there is a deep rest in the now.

THREE

Ending the War Within

"My invitation is revolutionary. It takes you to the razor's edge of mind and heart. Right here, if you are ruthlessly honest in staying open, you will die as the 'you' you think you are and be born into awakeness. And even if you are alive as this awakeness for one moment only, the revolution has begun. It is the end of the war of inner conflict. And the beginning of silence as the true song of your life."

Cleaning up Your Environment

Awakening has nothing to do with the achievement of a special state of consciousness. It has everything to do with presence and openness.

When you live as presence and openness—in all ways and always—you are the light of the world. You haven't achieved a special state of consciousness or become saintly, but something has been purified inside. It is your heart that is purified. It is purified because in presence and openness you are no longer projecting your unconscious beliefs onto the world. In other words, you are no longer coming to a conclusion about the world. By world, I mean everything—your intimate relationships, your work, your body, everything that you relate to, everything that you experience in your personal life as well as in the global collective situation.

When you come to conclusions about what you see, about what you feel, about what you experience, you are polluting the world. You are polluting the world because you are adding to the argument—you are adding to the division. When you come to a conclusion, you have to take a position. It's *this* position or *that* position. It's either a good position or a bad position. In this way, you add to the weight of divisiveness in the world.

When you meet the world without dividing it into good and bad pieces, when you simply meet the world without coming to a conclusion, there's no pollution. This doesn't mean you lose discernment. This doesn't mean you lose objective clear-seeing when you see injustice, when you see abuse—whether it's in your personal relationship or in the wider global arena. This doesn't mean you turn a blind eye and say, *"Well I'm not coming to a conclusion la, la, la."* No. It means you see and you feel—you let it penetrate you all the way. You let that injustice, that suffering penetrate you all the way so it pierces your heart open—and your heart remains open. From this place you can respond intelligently, not reactively.

When you react—when there's a knee-jerk conclusion—this is pollution, not truth. Truth is clear seeing and the absence of resistance to what is. From this place there is either movement—we can also call it intelligent response—or there is no movement, just stillness, just silence and the simplicity of an open heart. Movement or no movement—it's right action when it arises out of an inner environment that's free of the pollution of conclusion, position, or opinion.

This changes everything—this changes you, and it changes the world.

Transforming Reactivity

"I find myself being reactive when someone says or does something I don't like or agree with. This reactivity seems to create more problems in my life. It seems to happen automatically, without my involvement. Is there anything I can do to stop it?"

First of all, what's needed is not a *doing*, it's a *sensitivity*. It is not a matter of using force, but a matter of becoming aware of a different kind of power in you—the power of becoming sensitive to the posturing of self-righteousness. And only you can align yourself with this power . . . no one else can give it to you.

When you take up a position of certainty about how you've been wronged, how you've been hurt, how you've been misunderstood, how you've been ignored, how you've been unfairly treated or misrepresented or victimized in some way, this self-righteousness ends up as reactivity—a knee-jerk reaction to lash out, to attack, to retaliate, or to put up a barrage of defenses, to harden, to recoil. This mechanism is mostly unconscious, it seems to happen automatically. Very often you don't see it until some time after the reaction has happened, and then you berate yourself.

If you become sensitive to this self-righteousness—by meeting your experience without taking a position, by feeling more deeply into your experience, by being more honest with yourself as to what's happening inside you—then you will start to see it sooner and sooner. If you become sensitive, you will be able to stay on the razor's edge toward that self-righteousness, to just be here and not move with it when it springs up.

When you move from self-righteousness, you create suffering for yourself, because you're the one in pain, you're the one who is suffering in that self-righteousness. Most likely you also create suffering for those around you. When you become sensitive toward that mechanism of self-righteousness, you can see it rise up as if in slow-motion and there's a possibility of stopping right here. But there's no violence in this stopping . . . you can't force it. Stopping it is not about doing anything, it's not about applying your will. But in seeing clearly—and this is what being sensitive is about—the self that takes up a position is no longer there. It's as if the tight knot of self dissolves in the space of open awareness. And in this openness, there is a natural stop. No action is taken, either in your mind or in your body.

When the willful self is no longer there, something intelligent will move in you. Right action will move in you. Right action can be a movement or it can be no movement—either way it will be intelligent.

"Are you saying I should practice stillness?"

Very often we think that if we practice stillness or presence or silence in meditation or another deliberate spiritual practice, we can somehow replicate that stillness or presence in everyday life. We think we can bring it into our relationships, so that when we're triggered we can remain still or we can remain silent or remain present. But this is an error—you cannot impose your spiritual practice on life.

When you're triggered, it's not stillness that's being called for—it's openness. This openness requires a willingness for self-exposure—the willingness to expose yourself *to* yourself. What you are being invited to expose are the raw feelings, the ugly feelings, the scary feelings—whatever feelings you have spent a lifetime contorting yourself around to keep them hidden from yourself.

I don't mean you should express these feelings as an outburst of emotion, but rather to meet these feelings in the quiet space of your innermost—to listen to your inner truth and tell the truth to yourself about what you feel. It seems one of the scariest things—on a psychological level—is to meet ourselves all the way. So we create layers of armoring around our innermost feelings, we create layers of pretense. We don't meet ourselves all the way, we don't meet each other all the way, and we don't meet life all the way. The willingness to meet your experience all the way—to be honest with yourself about your feelings—softens the layers of pretense and defense. And in this softness you are less likely to be triggered, because you are open to a deeper truth. It is this openness that transforms reactivity to peace.

"But how can I trust life enough so I can open to it?"

Openness has nothing to do with trust. Trust implies that you know where you're going to land. If I start to open to you, or to life, or to the depths of my feelings, "trust" wants to know that I'll be okay, that there's a safety net. The need for a safety net means you are bargaining with life—if you give me love or success or comfort, then I will open. Well, you can try to bargain—and many people spend their whole lives bargaining with life! But bargaining doesn't lead to intimacy. It doesn't lead to love. And it doesn't lead to freedom.

True intimacy, true love, and true freedom demand that you give up all strategies, that you give up all attempts to bargain with life. You are called to give yourself as openness, without the demand or expectation for anything in return. Whether you trust or don't trust, that's irrelevant. This openness demands that you put down your weapons. These weapons are all the strategies, all the maneuvers, all the attempts to "be good" so that life rewards you with goodness, all the attempts to "be loving" so that the other loves you. While that sounds like an innocuous pastime, these strategies are weapons of war. They keep you in the realm of reactivity, caught in the matrix of defense and attack.

When you don't get what you think you deserve from life—whether it be love or recognition or success or security—the default option is to withhold yourself. You can use your weapons to create a barricade, to reject life. Or you can use your weapons to attack, to argue with reality. None of these strategies work—they only make the prison walls thicker and higher.

So, perhaps you can see now that the end of reactivity has nothing to do with spiritual practice—and everything to do with being willing to turn toward an inner gentleness. It's a gentleness toward your experience. You don't have to fight your experience. You don't have to reject it. You don't have to use it as an excuse to close down, an excuse to harden. Simply, and utterly, be gentle toward your innermost experience. That gentleness is toward the innermost and toward whatever you see and interact with. You don't need to become more compassionate or more patient or more spiritual. You don't need to be concerned with changing your behavior: your behavior will take care of itself.

The real transformation takes place when you give up your strategies of war.

Putting Down All Weapons of War

"Being gentle when something threatens me seems to be one of the most difficult things."

Yes, we're hardwired physiologically to be on alert. This is a necessary protection for the physical vehicle. When we are in a dark alley and we sense someone following us, our nervous system is highly attuned to the possibility of fighting the stalker or running away. Or when we are walking across the road and a car doesn't slow down, we are primed to react quickly to get out of the way. But we need to differentiate this *functional* alertness from psychological reactivity—which is an emotional response that has nothing to do with biological survival.

If something irritates us or frustrates us or agitates us or presses our buttons in some way, we're very quick to believe the righteousness of our feelings. Often we very quickly follow that up with feeling that we shouldn't feel so triggered by the situation; we berate ourselves for being reactive, and then we feel righteous about that! It's a never-ending cycle that hardens the shell of ego-self. It's a mental stance, a position the mind takes, flipping from *"I'm right"* to *"I'm wrong"* at the push of a button.

Gentleness means there is no avoidance of what is felt—the full depth and breadth of your inner experience comes into con-sciousness. You are fully aware of the feeling, but it doesn't stick to you as a sense of righteousness. Righteousness comes when a mental narrative wraps itself around the feeling: you argue, you fight, you reject, you tighten, you withdraw. Without the narra-tive, the feeling passes through your field of consciousness. It is simply experienced as an energy, a "felt-sense" without your commentary. There is no mental position in this, you have no place to land. Of course, without a landing place you are open and you feel vulnerable.

As you come to know yourself as this openness more and more, this sense of vulnerability dissolves. As you fall into your innermost nature as openness, you come to see that there's no real boundary between you and your experience. You come to realize that there's no "separate self" that needs to identify itself as vulnerable or not vulnerable—there's no "separate self" that needs to be protected. So there's no need to push away the truth of your inner experience.

As you come to know yourself as openness, love—not fear—becomes the primary driver of your life. When the mental posturing falls away, all that is left is the openness of love. *Love is the only thing that is real, everything else is imagined.*

This love is an unbounded inner dimension of being-ness. When you come to know your true nature as this being-ness, and come to rest in this always—because it is *always* here—you can stop doing any spiritual practice. There is nothing that can be added to this openness, nothing you can do that will improve this openness, nothing that can take you anywhere else than where you are *now*.

This openness is the perfection that includes everything— and this includes the imperfection of your human experience. Awakening is nothing other than this openness. The idea that awakening is a state of perpetual bliss—that you're lorded on a cloud as a rock star of the "spiritual kingdom" is absolute fantasy!

> *"I can understand the need to be kind and tender toward other people, especial-ly those we love. But I find it very difficult to be kind and tender toward myself."*

We are not often kind or tender toward ourselves—at least not at the deepest level. Sometimes we think we are being kind to ourselves, perhaps by treating ourselves to a soothing massage or something yummy to eat or a night in watching a movie. But if you examine this situation with honesty, you most likely are not listening to yourself with the utmost loving tenderness. It's not a matter of *what* you do, what actions you take to prove your love to yourself—it's a matter of whether you are truly listening to your innermost.

To listen to, to taste, to touch what arises in you in response to the ebb and flow of your life, your circumstances, your think-ing, your emotions, the dynamics of your psyche—as all these rise and fall and different parts come into view at different times—to *be with what arises* in the utmost tenderness means to not judge, to not control, to not attempt to fix, nor even to attempt to provide an answer. This is a subtle inner dimension of being. You may not like what arises, you may not like what is felt, but learning this art of conscious surrender is the only way to end the war within.

Just listen . . . which means just be open. You have the capacity, if you allow yourself, to meet what is here without any boundary, without any limit. Relax all attempts, all strategies, all mental and emotional acrobatics. When you relax all of that, what is here as the naked reality that's always unfolding and revealing itself—the nakedness of *this*, the nakedness of *this*, the nakedness of *this*—becomes your abiding home.

So it's not as if you arrive somewhere special. It's not that you suddenly "get" the ultimate truth. It's simply that the more you relax into *this*—into whatever arises as your experience—the openness reveals itself. The more you relax, the less you judge and the less you resist. And then—either in an instant, or with the passage of time—your natural state as openness which has always been in the background, comes into the foreground. It's a very natural process.

The Existential Abyss

"There are times when I surrender so deeply that an existential abyss appears. I feel a great terror here. I fear that I will not survive. I get the sense there is liberation on the other side, but I tighten up. What is the way through?"

There is no way through. You can't make it happen. You can't say, *"Well, if I push myself to the edge, to this place that's so scary, then somehow I'll jump over the fence and I will have arrived."* This statement is a big agenda that creates an even bigger contraction.

As long as you have an agenda, as long as you have an imagined destination, there is no real transformation of consciousness. This transformation isn't about understanding something or doing something or knowing something. It's about letting go of all of that sort of thing. Every moment offers the opportunity to let go of agenda and let go of hope. If there is a so-called path, then it's accepting the ongoing invitation from life to turn toward openness—*now* and *now* and *now*. The ongoing invitation is to notice whether there's a subtle (or not so subtle!) pull away from tenderly meeting the full depth of that which reveals itself. Even when there is resistance, the resistance can be met from a place of openness.

This ongoing invitation is really about allowing yourself to taste, to feel the texture of, to not shy away from, to not know where opening will take you or what will happen. When suffering is not wanted—whether it's physical pain or psychological pain—that's the time to get really close to get close to the experience of pain or contraction or resistance. That's the time to just enjoy the texture of the suffering. That's not the time to say, *"Well, if I was awakened, then I wouldn't be feeling this suffering."* That's not the time to embark on a trajectory of mind that searches for the ultimate awakened pain-free state. That is the wrong kind of inquiry. The only kind of inquiry that is worthwhile, is the kind that brings you closer to your experience not further away.

When this pain or this contraction or this resistance appears, this is the time to say *"Welcome! Thank you. Thank you for knocking on the door."* This suffering is not in opposition to the freedom you really want. Paradoxically, it is here to give you the opportunity to get close to your experience, to get intimate with it—not with your mind, not by understanding it, but by meeting it more deeply. You're familiar with the stories—you know what happened in the past, you know the circumstances that caused suffering. Accepting the ongoing invitation is not about remembering your history, it's not about digging into your memory banks and regurgitating the pain. It's about getting close to the pain or the contraction or the resistance from the inside. It's about meeting your experience from the deep—from the deep that has no name, from the deep that has no understanding, from the deep that has no strategy or method or path.

And only *you* have the capacity to say *yes* to that. You are required to be vigilant in this *yes*. It's not a matter of just saying, *"I'm aware of this feeling, this memory, this sensation,"* and just leaving it at that. Vigilance is the tenacity to come even closer to what is here in your experience, to come closer to the energetic layers inside the feeling, inside the memory, inside the sensation . . . and to come even closer to the wide open awareness that holds it all.

This is the art of conscious surrender—and it has ever deeper dimensions, ever more subtle dimensions. Wherever you are—whatever is happening or not happening, whatever your experience, whatever your understanding or revelations or insights—there is still more depth and more closeness available. Because that which appears as life never ends.

Seeing the Mechanism of Separation

"I have been meditating for over forty years,
and still I have a sense of separation. It seems my
spiritual practice has come to naught. How can
I know oneness?"

Spiritual practice on its own is not enough. It's not enough to practice meditation or mindfulness or to achieve a state of unity during your spiritual practice but then revert to the habitual paradigm of separation in your everyday life. The whole of your life should be a living inquiry. Not as an intellectual exercise that leads you to examine every thought and every feeling (that would be exhausting!), but a living inquiry in the sense of *becoming sensitive* to how the mechanism of separation is the driving force in the relationship to yourself and in your relationship to the world. Let's explore this a little further . . .

You are constantly in relationship: there is a *subject* and an *object*. You are the subject. And whatever arises in your field of consciousness is the object—in other words, every thought, every feeling, every sensation. You are constantly in relationship to this object. However, this relationship is mostly unconscious, as are most relationships. You're either moving toward the object in order to lose yourself in it or possess it, or you're running away from it in order to avoid it or reject it or overpower it. And in this moving toward or moving away, you live in a divided state in which there are seemingly two: you, and whatever is happening to you.

A living inquiry begins with the willingness to see the mechanism of moving toward and moving away, to become sensitive to that mechanism. When you're willing to expose the bare facts of your experience, you then have the opportunity to investigate what is really true—what is naked reality, and what is imagination. Naked reality is always a "felt-sense," unembellished and uncontrived. The imagination of it is the narrative you create around your experience—and this always has an element of judgement or grievance in it.

The mechanism of separation plays out in many ways in our everyday lives. There are many subtle strategies that perpetuate an unconscious relationship to life. Take the example of something that seems very innocuous, such as habitually watching movies or listening to the radio or snacking, or even something seemingly altruistic like the urge to help a friend by giving advice or chatting on the phone with them. Very often what underlies these actions is an unconscious movement away from ourselves. An impulse arises to do something and we naturally follow this impulse. There's nothing wrong with taking action or "doing something" when it serves a function. But very often the action is motivated by an unconscious fear of being truly intimate with the bare truth of our experience.

The bare truth is that we are scared to death of meeting our core sense of separation, so we do anything to avoid this fear. On a subtle level, the avoidance may appear as the compulsion to fix a friend's problems. On a more obvious level, it may be the addiction to food or cigarettes or chemical intoxication. What's happening here is the attempt to merge with the object of our doing so that we can feel complete.

There's an existential wound that each of us carries simply because of having been born into form and separated from the oceanic womb of consciousness. When this wound is not embraced consciously, we live from a sense of "me" as a separate entity. And as a separate entity, there's a compulsion to move toward or merge with whatever object appears in our field of consciousness. It could be a thought, a feeling, an object of desire, or an activity that seems to satisfy us.

I'm calling it a wound, but it's not really a wound. It's an *imagined* wound—a core belief which creates a psychological structure around separation. We experience this core belief as a sense of alone-ness or a sense of abandonment or a sense of emptiness—something not quite yet fulfilled. On the surface, the attempt to find this fulfillment ends up as various behaviors or actions. Perhaps you become a film star or pop star, voracious for adulation. Perhaps you become an alcoholic or a drug addict, driven by the longing of oblivion. Perhaps you become addicted to helping others, because you don't want to face your alone-ness. Or perhaps you are addicted to being in love, constantly looking for completion through the perfect relationship. All of these patterns are the end-result of not facing the core struc-ture of self that believes itself to be a separate entity. When the attempt to find fulfillment from things you "do" and "have" loses its allure, it's very likely that a deeper sense of empti-ness—a pervading sense of abandonment or alone-ness that is unattached to the circumstances of your life—starts to reveal itself. But far from this being a problem, this is wonderful . . . here is the opportunity to see through the illusion of separation. So, don't reject this emptiness—welcome it!

In my life, there were two things that had this kind of uncon-scious pull on me. One was the impulse to make myself a cup of tea or a sweet treat when I was sitting alone in my living room. The other was to read an uplifting spiritual book when I felt in need of hope and solace. Even though these activities were harmless in themselves, they strengthened the sense of "me" as a separate entity by avoiding the meeting of an existential aloneness that revealed itself whenever I was still. The movement of mind that urged me to take action—making a cup of tea or reading a spiritual book—was an avoidance of facing the terror of this aloneness.

For some reason—you may call it grace or you may call it karma—I was given the possibility to clearly see the mech-anism of separation playing itself out. It was like watching in slow motion the movement of mind followed by the impulse of desire and then followed by movement of the body toward an end result. And in this clear-seeing, I was given the possibility to just stop and not follow that movement of thought, not follow that impulse of desire, and not take any action at all. The whole scene—from thinking to desire to action to result—was seemingly harmless; but the clear-seeing of that trajectory was a replay of an ancient momentum that permeated and upheld the egoic structure of separation. I knew in that moment that this mechanism was the root cause of psychological suffering.

So I stopped going along with it. This stopping wasn't an overpowering of the mechanism, there was no force used. There was just something—you might call it awareness—that saw the futility and the exhaustion of following that compulsion. It's the same when we follow the movement of thoughts, especially when it's about dreaming of the future—when we hope for more love or more success or more happiness, when we dream of a better life and a better world in which everything is perfect and only good things come to us. This seeking of fulfillment in an imagined future is a common trait of the separate "me" or egoic self. And it was a tenacious compulsion of mine too.

When we stop following the movement of mind that seeks fulfillment in a future moment, a kind of abyss opens up. And in that abyss a great terror arises, an existential fear that the "me" I hang my whole life on is actually just a blip in the totality of existence. If we have the courage and the awareness to just hang out here, to stay suspended in "not knowing," not trying to find any ground or conclusion, we might just see that who I think I am—the separate "me" that I defend at all costs—is a complete figment of the imagination. When we have the courage to face the bare reality of the blip, an energetic knot that we've been caught up in for the whole of our lives simply dissolves—in other words, our world falls apart. This dissolving, this falling apart, is freedom. And this freedom is often experienced as an "aha!" It can be very profound, or it can be very subtle.

The practice of meditation is often a necessary entry-point

into seeing this movement of mind, and a great support on the journey of awakening out of the dream of separation. But meditation in itself is not enough—there needs to be a living inquiry as well. A living inquiry is not a practice you set time aside for and then forget about: it is an ongoing way of relating to your experience of life. To live in this way, there needs to be the willingness to see, to become sensitive to the movement of mind. Developing this sensitivity is not about behavioral control, it's not about overpowering your mind. It's a slowing down. When we slow down, we fall into an inner silence. And in this inner silence—which is the same as inner wholeness—any core beliefs about ourselves that are not aligned to this silence or wholeness are highlighted. The most common belief that gets brought into the glaring headlights is the core belief that *"I am separate,"* and with it the experience of a sense of abandonment or rejection or unworthiness or unlovability. Right here, in the midst of the horror of this experience, we are given an opportunity to wake up out the dream of separation.

If we have the courage to tenderly be *with* that sense of unlovability or rejection or abandonment *without* the narrative about it—the narrative that insists that I feel this rejection because my parents abandoned me, because my lover left me, because I've lost my dog, or any other seemingly valid reason—there is the possibility to recognize what is here prior to any thought. We are offered an opportunity to fall into the silence of awareness, the background of the movie of "my life," the ever-present space within which everything appears and disappears. We are offered the possibility to see and sense that which is completely untouched, that which cannot be divided, that which is—and never was—separate from the totality of existence.

Everything in our lives is a doorway to waking up out of the dream of separation. Nothing is too small or too ordinary to be investigated. Very often we push aside our human experience, either believing it's something we need to fix or something we need to ignore while we focus on the very important task of spiritual practice. True spiritual practice acknowledges that the human experience of pain and suffering is a potent doorway to freedom if we have the courage to meet it all the way—to sit inside it without a narrative, to taste it without interpretation or interference. But even though the human experience is included, it's not about the self "fixing itself," and neither is it about the self "having a spiritual insight." Waking up out of the dream of separation is about seeing what is more primary—more intimate and ever-present—than the separate self that's trying to do anything or get anything.

Everything in your life—every experience and every relationship—is a doorway to realizing your true nature as oneness.

When Feelings Stop Being the Enemy

"I used to think that I had to be strong in order to overcome negative feelings. But I'm seeing now that this is the wrong approach."

Openness is not a weakness. It's a quietness. Even if there is agitation, there can be inner quiet. In quietness, you're not fighting the agitation. You're not trying to smash it down, to stomp on it by saying, *"This shouldn't be here."* In quietness, your response to the agitation is gentle, but it's not weak. On the contrary, this quietness is your invincibility—because from this quietness you move courageously through life. It's not the kind of courage the ego-self understands, it's not the kind of courage which requires you to do something that proves your strength—you don't have to shoot down the enemy.

At the root of all emotions and feelings we don't like or

want is fear. Fear is our greatest enemy. Fear is what we really don't want to face. But the courage to face fear doesn't mean you should drag yourself to the edge of the cliff and then force yourself to jump. The true courage to face fear comes from quietly coming close to what scares you—and smiling at it. It's like standing at the edge and gently letting go of the tight grip. It's not the same as taking a leap—you don't have to run and jump. It's just gently letting go of the grip. It's an inner smile, an openness that befriends everything. In openness, you are invincible—there is nothing, not even your greatest fear, that needs to be turned away from.

As long as there is some part of your experience that is seen as the enemy, there can be no real union with existence, there can be no lasting realization of your true nature as wholeness. You may have reached extraordinary states of *samadhi*, you may have a mind-blowing glimpse into the nature of reality, you may have experienced an incredible silence in deep meditation—but as long as you make an enemy of any part of your experience, there can be no abiding sense of oneness with yourself or with life.

True awakening—awakening that is lived as an everyday reality—takes place when every vestige of separation between you and life comes to an end. Of course, when you operate in the world, there is the appearance of a separate body that must be honored, taken care of, and so on. This perceived separation is functional—it's a necessary aspect of our physiology, if we are to survive and thrive as individuations of the "one life." But identifying solely with this functional or physiological aspect of life is the root cause of our psychological suffering. If we are to awaken out of this dream, the imagined separation between "me" and "life" must come to an end.

When you no longer see an enemy in any part of your human

experience, you're onto something! Without an enemy, awakening will inevitably flower in you. You don't have to do anything. You don't have to understand anything. You don't have to achieve anything. This awakening may not be a "high" experience or a mind-blowing experience—but it will be the flowering of love.

From love, there is power. There is the power of the intelligence of life. It's an invisible power that becomes amplified as more and more individuations of the "one life" remember their true nature as that love.

"What does this love look like? And how can it change the world?"

It's a quiet love, an undefended state, that has nothing to do with behavior or expression. It has nothing to do with being a nice person or a loving person or a spiritual person. Although, in undefended-ness, the love that you are in your innermost will percolate into your mind-body vehicle and quieten your nervous system. Most likely this will give rise to the expression of kindness, generosity and compassion. But it's not up to you to decide what your behavior should look like—it will happen naturally without the overlay of spiritual ideology or principles.

When you are focused on what it looks like to be a spiritual person or to be a compassionate person or to be a loving person or to be a good person, you interfere with the natural flow of innate goodness from your innermost. But when you simply attend to putting down all psychological weapons of war when faced with an uncomfortable or scary feeling, an inner wellspring of being-ness and love—of goodness and God-ness—will inevitably, naturally, organically, and quietly flow into you and infuse your life.

If you could turn your attention to this one inner action of becoming sensitive to where the inner war is still operating in you and say, *"Yes, I'm willing to put down my weapons of war in response to this experience,"* then everything else in you will be taken care of. True nature will reveal itself, either gradually or suddenly (it doesn't matter, either way). You can relax, and you can stop being concerned with achieving a higher state of consciousness or with changing the world. Just simply, and utterly, give your attention to ending the war within.

True power—the power to respond intelligently—comes from a much deeper source than the surface mind that wants to fix what's wrong, that wants to mend what's broken, that wants to change the world. True power arises naturally when you look within and go to the source of all that is broken. You will find that deeper than the world and its brokenness are your thoughts about the world. Action based on thoughts that arise from separation is the root of war. Action based on thoughts that arise from the wholeness of true nature is the seed of peace. Right action—not self-righteous action—always takes place from quiet openness.

Look within, and know yourself as this openness. This is the way of peace.

FOUR

The Intelligence of Love

"Love is a force that moves in us as natural intelligence, the kind of intelligence that takes care of the whole not just the individual parts. It takes care of the whole body, the whole human being, the whole society, the whole nation, the whole world."

Love Calls You All the Way Home

There is an intelligence at the core of life, an intelligence that drives the trajectory of our lives. If you would recognize it, it would bring you all the way home to love.

You can't truly know this love until you meet the existential terror of being totally alone. Aloneness is the final frontier to the love that is life itself. Each and every one of us carries this existential aloneness—we are each born alone and we each die alone. It doesn't matter whether we are surrounded by loving friends/family/parents or whether we are alone and destitute in a jail cell, we still have to meet our existential aloneness at these times. Both are very intimate affairs, a relationship between the self and God. Most people don't acknowledge this existential fact, but instead sugarcoat these two most important journeys.

Every one of us—saint and sinner, mother and murderer—is expelled from the womb of oneness through the act of birth, and every one of us is forced to let go of life as we know it at the moment of death. At some point in our lives, this terror of aloneness reveals itself—perhaps when the body falls apart due to illness or aging, or when our finances show a big drop in income or savings, or when the well of enthusiasm and inspiration dries up in our work and creativity, or when a beloved spouse or child or pet leaves us.

We can find this wound of separation in every aspect of the human experience. It is like a crack or thread that runs between life and death, between form and formless, between fullness and emptiness—and through every aspect of the human experience. We can begin to heal this separation when we finally admit to ourselves that there is fear or struggle or a sense of unworthiness in our lives. We begin to heal it when we're honest about where and how it plays itself out in our relationship to ourselves, in our relationship to others, and in our relationship to the world. We find it in the places where we suffer—because suffering is always an indicator of an inner division.

The embodiment of awakening requires us to see how this inner division underlies many of our feelings, our decisions, and our actions. Nothing is too unspiritual to be included in our journey of awakening. Awakening doesn't take us off into another realm where we transcend the human experience. It doesn't magically make the human experience perfect. It doesn't mean that the trajectory of your life suddenly comes to a full stop and you live in an enlightened stratosphere. It means that everything in your life that was previously in the shadows comes rushing in to be seen and healed and resolved in love, to be held in honesty and intimacy. And this means *everything*—including the darkest, most challenging, most painful feelings. Everything is the Beloved in disguise. It is only you that separates the Beloved into an image of perfection and then banishes anything that isn't aligned with that image. The Beloved *is* everything.

God is in everything. God is in the fullness of what is here *as your experience*—including rage, resentment, and regret. Fullness doesn't mean you draw the darkness into yourself and hold onto it—you don't have to take possession of rage and create a false god out of it. Rage—or resentment or regret, or anything else—is just the doorway to God. When you simply meet it with tenderness, it comes rushing in to your heart and dissolves into acceptance. When rage or irritation or disappointment or brokenness or worthlessness—whatever it is that that you're running away from—is no longer met by the hard wall of judgment, it comes to rest in the emptiness of awareness. It resolves itself, back into love. That love isn't the love *of* something, but the purity of love as the space of consciousness without content.

Everything is the intelligence of love—calling you all the way home.

"I am confused about the relationship
between emptiness and fullness. Isn't non-
dual awareness the realization of emptiness
as the ground of reality, and isn't this what I
should be striving for on my spiritual path?"

True awakening means the conversation about achieving a spiritual state collapses. Living the truth of awakening means there is no more division between being spiritual and being unspiritual. If humanity is going to evolve, we must take this conversation a little bit further than simply trying to realize non-dual awareness.

Yes, go inside. Yes, go right up to the void—go right up to that edge where mind can no longer carry you. Stand at that edge and allow the psychological knot of self to be annihilated.

Yes, go all the way into the void—without this annihilation of self, there is no transformation of consciousness. But after the internal structure of self has fallen away, allow the world as it filters into your life to enter all the way. Allow this to be a further purification, because however deep or profound or all-encompassing your non-dual realization there is still a backlog of human karma that you've dragged along with you into this moment, and it says, *"What about me? Am I loved too?"*

All of that backlog comes rushing in to be purified in the light of awakeness. It doesn't just get left behind—there's no dumping ground for your rubbish. You may have woken up out of your story, you may have realized the essential emptiness of consciousness—but there's still a bag of unexamined, unwelcomed energies that previously were unmet. For reasons that were appropriate at the time, they got shoved into the shadows, presumed dead. But they're still alive and knocking on the door, from the inside. These energies are yearning to be met *now*, to be purified in the light of the awakeness that has been born in you.

When this purification process has burnt away all resistance, you can live fully awake *and* fully human. Fully human means that you are rooted right *here* and everything—the whole mess *and* the whole beauty—is pouring through you. It's alive, it's present, it's unending. And as long as *you* are alive and fully awake, you are not in denial of your experience. There's no avoidance, no contortion—you are not creating mental and emotional acrobatics around your experience. It is simply *as it is*. And your response to what is becomes *right action*.

When you stop fighting and arguing with your experience, you can move in the world from an undivided state. It doesn't mean you become a passive, peaceful, enlightened caricature of yourself. Sometimes the movement is wrathful—you (metaphorically) pick up a sword and chop off the head of the one who attempts to harm you (or harm someone else) either physically or psychically. You are like a Samurai warrior in the midst of a battlefield, able to slay the enemy without being attached to either a personal sense of victory or vanquish. And sometimes that movement has no movement in it at all—it is so still you can't find the world in it. You become like a yogi sitting in a cave and being bitten by mosquitoes and remaining in peace. Either way—action or non-action—when it arises as the song of silence, it is love.

> *"Often, when I experience a deep opening to love, it is followed by a closure into fear. I don't understand why this happens."*

When there has been a deep or profound opening, everything that is unlike itself will come into view. When there is an opening to love, everything that is the opposite of that comes in to be seen and to be held in that love.

It is not here as a punishment, it is not here because you've done something wrong. It is here to be seen and held in the lightness of being—which is the same as love—because everything yearns to come home. The fear yearns to come home, the rejection yearns to come home, everything that you can name as an energetic experience yearns to come home to source. The source is the open spaciousness of being—which is the same as love.

Your job is to *be* that open space which allows it to come home. It is arrogant and unkind to reject the energy that wants to come home to itself as love *in* you. An unloved energy has no other way to come home—it can only do that through the portal of conscious awareness. And only *you* have the capacity for meeting it there and welcoming it home.

A chair can't be a portal for love, because the chair hasn't developed the capacity for conscious awareness. Only you as a human being have the capacity for self-reflection and therefore can be conscious of what has been trapped in the shadows of unconsciousness. When there has been an opening—either in a deep state of meditation, or with the support of a psycho-spiritual practice, or in the presence of profound beauty—whatever was previously unloved has the opportunity to come home. It knocks or pounds or bangs on the door of your heart. If you meet its energy with fear, you will experience a closure. But if you welcome it, it dissolves back into the infinite consciousness whence it was born.

So to be that open space—come what may—is an act of kindness, an act of love, an act of service.

Deeper than Mind

"Can you say something about grace? My understanding is that grace is an invisible force that guides and supports us on our spiritual journey."

Grace is one of those words that often conjures up images of only good things happening to us. I invite you to expand your view of grace.

Every feeling we have is a child of God, yearning to come home to the lightness of an open hand of love. When it sits lightly in the open hand, there is no attempt to reject it or to hold on to it—it has come home to love. This means that the feeling passes through you more quickly, because it has nothing to stick to. It falls into openness, and this falling into openness is grace.

Grace is the movement of life when it flows through you, unimpeded by you. In this openness, everything is given to you—birth and death, gain and loss, pain and pleasure—all of it moves through you gracefully. In moving through the open vessel of an undefended self—a self in which the rigid shell of resistance and self-righteousness and erroneous self-beliefs about being abandoned or rejected or punished by life, has fallen away—all of it is experienced as the exquisite richness of life.

Both agony and ecstasy are exquisitely rich. Consider this— whatever you experience is never to be repeated. Each moment (if we could dissect the eternal moment into moments) is never repeated. Contemplate this, feel this—let it sink in. It is never repeated! Every time you reject an experience and deny it by saying, *"This is not good enough, this shouldn't have happened,"* you reject the gift of that moment. It is never going to be repeated— you have missed it, just by waiting for the perfect moment. This is a siphoning away of aliveness.

By truly cherishing each moment—not by possessing it or owning it or making it special so that you can feel special about yourself but by just being with it, by holding it lightly, by meeting it all the way, by honoring its very existence in this moment—it can flow through you. Whether there are mountains or vales, whether you walk through the valley of darkness or fly through the heavens of light, it's all grace—*all* of it. And yet we often miss that opportunity by creating mental imaginings of how life should be, images about what I should be feeling or experiencing in order to have a better life.

I invite you to abandon or throw away all *shoulds* and *shouldn'ts* and instead really taste what's here—really take it in. In this way, you will be nourished by life. When you are eating and you really taste the food, it gets metabolized into nourishment, into fuel for life. And so it is with life itself, so it is with every experience you have.

If you don't taste what life offers, it doesn't get metabolized into love, it doesn't get transformed into grace, and you don't feel nourished by life. So then you go looking for nourishment elsewhere—from your relationships, from your work, from your possessions, from the accumulation of wealth or recognition or knowledge.

There's nothing wrong with any of these things in themselves—they are expressions of life—but looking for nourishment in the world of form doesn't bring lasting fulfillment. Looking for fulfillment in the world of form leads to codependent relationships. A codependent relationship is one in which you're seeking something in order to know yourself as something—you seek love from a relationship in order to feel loved or to feel lovable. You have turned love into a commodity, something that you can give and receive—and this is not true love. It's the same with recognition or approval. When you seek approval or recognition or worthiness from the work you do or from the creativity you pursue or from any activity, your relationship to that becomes a codependent one—you need to keep doing it in order to feel fulfilled, at least temporarily.

But when you are truly nourished by the aliveness of each moment, there is no codependency—there is no give and take, there is no need, there is no expectation. There is only oneness with life itself. This alive presence is the source of true nourishment. There is fullness, and yet you are empty of self. This is true fulfillment.

"I often feel confusion or conflict when trying to make decisions or take actions. Is there an intelligence that is deeper than mind?"

The mind that has not yet awakened to its true nature is always in a divided state—*"This is good and this is bad," "This matches up to my expectations but this doesn't," "I can take ownership of this experience but this one I will reject,"* and so on. Mind compartmentalizes and categorizes experiences based on past memory and future imagination, and so life becomes divided into fear and hope. This division is a cause of great conflict in us. Nothing truly intelligent can arise out of this conflict.

The resolution to this conflict is to turn toward something more true than the mind's habit of compartmentalizing. You already know what is more true in the depth of you, in your innermost. You don't know it with your mind—no understanding or knowledge can take you there. But you know it in the unspoken realm of the heart, in the depth of undefended silence that is your innermost. This is the undivided state of being. It is this that you long for—it is here that you can give your mind a rest and be informed by the natural flow of intelligence. It's a quiet space within, deeper and more tender than anything the mind can know.

When you fall into being-ness, you realize that it is not limited to the individual person. It's not *my* being—it doesn't belong to me. I cannot contain it. It's not that there is a multitude of being-nesses—there's only one, and this is at the core of everything that exists and everything that is experienced. It's the same with the intelligence that's deeper than mind—it's not limited or contained by the individual person, it can't belong to you. But it does have to come through you as an individual, in order to be known.

While this unbounded intelligence of the deep heart is already known to you in your innermost, there is often a journey of unpacking the armoring of the heart to be undertaken before this intelligence can truly flow in you. I call this journey "the crucifixion." As we turn away from listening to the mind's incessant compartmentalizing of experience and turn toward listening to a deeper truth, we encounter the fortresses we erected over a lifetime to protect us from unwanted feelings. These fortresses are refusals to meet the rawness of pain or fear without creating a narrative about it. At some point on the journey toward a deeper truth, we're called to make a choice—to reify the refusal, or to forge a new path of willingness. If we are truly willing to be crucified by what scares us, if we are truly willing to be broken open, there is a resurrection into love—into the unbrokenness of the true heart.

The true heart, the deep heart, is in fact invincible—but not in the way the ego wants to be. Not because it arms itself with an array of weapons—although the armoring or defendedness around the heart is an attempt to do that—but because its true nature, beneath the armoring, is openness, and openness cannot be cut in two. How could you break openness? How could you divide openness? By its very nature, openness is indivisible. By its very nature, openness has no boundary. It is limitless, just like the sky.

The true heart is undefended, and this undefendedness is your invincibility. To the mind, being undefended implies a vulnerability. And yes, there *is* a vulnerability—when we first touch this openness it feels as if there's nothing certain to stand on, there's no landing place we can rely on, there's no position we can take. So this vulnerability brings us to shaky ground. But as we come to trust this vulnerability more and more, we discover it is our invulnerability. In openness, nothing can touch you or harm you, not even death. Whatever you're experiencing in any circumstance, in any situation—whether you're in the marketplace of life, in the intensity of a relationship, or with the starkness of your aloneness—this openness is an invitation to end an ancient mechanism that creates the story of separation.

Openness invites you to fall into yourself as life itself. It's not a falling down into something, but a falling open. In this openness, self as a "separate entity in the vast eternity of existence" comes to an end. And when "you"—as the separate entity you believed yourself to be—come to an end, you know yourself as that which is timeless and eternal. You literally—viscerally—experience yourself as unlocalized, unconfined, untethered. This sounds scary to the mind, but it is freedom for the being. Of course, there is still a body that functions, still a personality that functions, still a human experience. But something has unequivocally come to an end.

On a practical level, how do you come to recognize the difference between the impulse to move from an undivided intelligence and the impulse to move from a self identified with separation? It's in the making of everyday decisions—*"Should I do this?" "Should I do that?" "How should I respond?"* and so on—that you can fine-tune a natural discernment of that difference. Initially, it seems like you have to apply some effort to this discernment, a kind of effort to be sensitive to whether the decision comes from surface mind or comes from deeper being-ness. Eventually, it becomes totally natural and the "right decision" seemingly arises by itself.

But while you're still in the navigation or discernment process, the clue to knowing which direction to take is to notice if there's an agenda attached to your decision-making—a strongly desired outcome, a demand that life lives up to your expectations, a sense that you are in control of your destiny. By sensing the tightness of your grip, you are likely to see how hooked up you are with the personal self. When you start becoming sensitive to your agendas—to the subtle but pervasive strategies of bartering, begging, and bullying life to give you what you want—this is the time to willingly surrender the agenda. It's as simple and as difficult as that!

First of all, admit that you don't know what the best outcome is for yourself or for anyone else or for the world. Recognize that the idea of knowing what is the best outcome lives only in the mind's imagination—an imagined future that pulls you away from the power of now. And then surrender any knowing from the mind, surrender any expectation—surrender any agenda. This surrender is a "hanging out in the unknown," neither saying *yes* nor saying *no* but surfing the edge of that part of you that wants to take a position in the matter.

Just "hang out" . . . wait.

Wait, without flapping around for an answer—without scrambling for something known. By waiting in the unknown, something will move you. It either will move you to keep absolutely still or it will move you to take action. This movement comes from a different place than the self who wants to control life— it's a quiet movement, unpolluted by past or future. And if you feel no movement either to be still or to take action, then keep waiting in the unknown.

This is how you develop the art of listening to a deeper intelligence.

"I have experienced many 'aha' experiences, moments of seeming realizations of absolute truth, but still this openness you speak of eludes me. Am I missing something?"

So often on the spiritual path we're caught up in looking for the "aha" experience—that mythical moment when we have the absolute realization of truth. These kinds of experiences may give us a glimpse of an awakened consciousness, but inevitably they come and go. True awakening—that filters into your whole life and way of being—is not something the mind can possess or understand.

In putting our attention on the desire for a transcendent state of mind that proves we have the precious trophy of awakening in our hands, we miss something very simple and very direct that is available to us right here and now—the softness of the heart.

This softness is available to you when you turn toward the innermost depths of what you know in your heart to be true—not what you know with the mind, but what the heart itself knows. The heart in its depth knows only one thing—softness and openness. Softness and openness are the same thing. It knows that only, and that's what I'm pointing to when I say "what your heart knows to be true."

But let's be very clear here—it's not about how you *feel* about something, it's not about your emotions. Very often we equate the word "heart" with how we feel—we feel hurt or rejected, or we feel joyful or loved. The heart that feels on a personal level is the outer heart, the surface dimension of the heart. I'm talking about something much deeper than that—I'm talking about the innermost. And this innermost is always available to you. The pull of form—whether it be the physical form of the body or the psychological form of thought—is toward hardness, tightness, self-righteousness, separation. But every moment of that seeming hardness and tightness and argument and resistance, holds within it—in its depth—an openness and softness. When that openness and softness of heart flows into your experience of form, you've woken up out of the dream of separation, at least for a moment.

When you feel hurt by someone's words or actions—when you feel insulted or aggrieved—you feel righteous about your feeling. You are absolutely sure that you've been hurt, that you've been insulted, that you've been aggrieved, that you've been abused. You invest yourself in upholding this righteousness. What you're really upholding is a mental stance, a kind of hardness. Inside this hardness is an invitation that is easily missed—the invitation to give yourself to the heart's deepest desire and knowing. This invitation is from the Beloved—it's the invitation from love, an invitation from the wholeness of your true nature.

On the surface, you want to be right. But in your depth, you want love and you want wholeness—you want to come home to rest in being. In those moments of tension, in those moments of conflict, in those moments of struggle and resistance, it seems the most difficult thing to turn toward that softness, to give yourself to the tenderness. But it's actually very simple. Love is very simple. Love is an openness that doesn't expect anything in return. Love is not a weakness, but a tenderness—and this distinction is difficult for the mind to understand.

If you could give up the search for an "aha" experience, if you could give up the search for "absolute truth" and simply turn your attention to love—you would be onto something good and real and true. I'm not talking about the kind of love you get from someone, the kind of love that makes you feel taken care of, or about the image of yourself as a loving person—but the love that is an infinite openness, an openness that has no expectation and no agenda but is simply itself. If you could turn toward this openness, toward this tenderness and this relaxation in every instance of righteousness, you would softly awaken to your true nature as love.

At the deepest level, love and truth are one. Truth is not a mental realization. Truth is what is here as the openness that is unobstructed by your need to defend your righteousness. In this openness you see clearly. You do not see argument, you do not see abuse, you do not see victim, you do not see enemy. You see love, because you *are* love.

As this love moves from your innermost into your human form, what you do becomes love in action. And this has nothing to do with conforming to your idea of what being loving looks like. Love in action is free of imagination.

Purity of the Heart

"Is the heart essentially pure? And does this purity have an impact on the expression of our human lives?"

The unbounded, infinite openness of the innermost—the depth of the heart—is pure. There is a natural wholesomeness, a natural clarity. When this moves into your life, it purifies the expression of your human vehicle. It doesn't make you a "perfect person," in the sense of conforming to your image of perfection. But it does clean up your thinking and your feeling, because it purifies your nervous system which has been encrusted with reactivity. When the nervous system is purified—when it calms down— everything comes into right alignment. There's a relaxing of defenses. There's a relaxing of trying to get more love or more power or more recognition or more self-worth from anyone or anything. In this relaxation, you come home to yourself.

Does this change the circumstances of your life? Does it change the experience of loss or hardship in life? Most probably, some situations in your life—certain relationships or activities that uphold and strengthen the reactivity of your nervous sys- tem—will fall away. They will no longer be interesting to you, or tenable. Either you will walk away, or they will walk away. But the waves of life—the gains and losses, the successes and failures, the heartbreaks—you can't control. What does change, though, is the attempt to get rid of anything—the attempt to control or fix or deny the bare fact of your human experience.

The argument with life seems very important to us while we're alive, but at death (and probably after death) the argument is no longer interesting to us and it comes to an end. The invitation offered here is to end that argument while you're still alive—because what the heart really knows is that which was here before the argument ever started. A life lived as tenderness, a life lived as openness is the absolute fulfillment.

The heart is infinite—like a bottomless well. The heart can absorb and allow everything—including what you perceive as a grievance, as an attack, as an offense. The heart doesn't reject anything; neither does it invest itself in anything. Everything can be thrown into that well, and in that tenderness it is purified. You don't have to do anything with it—you don't have to fix it, you don't have to process it. That one simple action of turning toward tenderness is the end of the offense. Of course, there may be layers to the issue. There may be something inside or underneath what first came up—another layer of feeling, perhaps a sense of rejection or abandonment or despair. But if you take this one key of turning toward tenderness, your life will be turned inside out by the purity and transformative power of love.

The whole of your life from birth to death is an opportunity for this transformation. Many people struggle with seeking their life's purpose—what direction to take in life, what to do or what to create or what to manifest in order to be truly fulfilled. The solution is simple, but commonly overlooked—your life's purpose is for the love that you already are to infuse your human form and experience, to infuse the manifestation of *you*. Everything else is secondary. What you *do* in your life will naturally flow out of the love that has infused you. When you give yourself to love, the struggle and striving for finding your purpose falls away.

It's a cleaning up of your act. As far as you know, you—as who you are in *this* form with *this* mind-body vehicle, with this personality, with *this* configuration of physiology and biology, with *these* circumstances that you have been born into, with *this* particular geometry that you call your life—only exist once. This specific lifetime cannot be repeated. And *you*—as this specific incarnation—are offered the chance to recognize the infinite openness in which your life arises and upon which the appearance of *you* utterly depends. Don't miss this opportunity!

Right Relationship

"Does the mind have any useful role in the human life?"

Very often on the spiritual path, it seems as if we're denigrating the mind or trying to get rid of it. But there's nothing wrong with the mind itself—it has its rightful place and is very useful.

Without the mind, you wouldn't have any discernment. The mind's true function is to compare, to contrast, to categorize, to compartmentalize. This is how you can function in three-dimensional reality, in the world of form. On a physiological level, you have to be able to see contrast—this gives you a perception that there are boundaries, separate forms in space. Without this capacity, you would not be able to make sense of your environment and you would not survive as a physical form.

The problem with the mind is that we've given all our power to the *movement* of mind. We've given allegiance to the *movement* of mind, not to the *nature* of mind—these are two different features of mind.

The *movement* of mind is the incessant stream of thinking that runs our lives in the "unconscious" state—this is the current state of the majority of humanity. Most people believe that if a thought arises it must be true and then they act on it, either by following it into an imaginary future or by getting rid of the past problem that led to this thought. Giving allegiance to the movement of mind is like the chasing the waves on the ocean—it's exhausting and doesn't lead to clarity . . . or sanity!

Truth cannot be found in the ever-changing nature of the waves. Only by penetrating the deeper nature of the waves can we know the wisdom of our innate wholeness—the ocean of being-ness. By recognizing that the ocean contains the wave but is not limited by the wave, we also recognize that being-ness contains thought but is not limited by thought. This realization changes the function of mind—it stops being the source of incessant suffering and comes into its rightful place to serve as a vehicle for the recognition of awareness—we call this "waking up to true nature" or "awakening out of the dream of separation."

In awakening out of the dream of separation—whether temporarily as a glimpse of oneness or permanently as a lived truth—the mind then continues to function when needed. It's a tool for "right action" in the three-dimensional world—but it's a tool we can pick up and put down. It's a useful function of mind to plan, to map, to focus, to concentrate. It's not useful to plan when you're just following some insane compulsion thought after thought after thought—but when mind falls into its rightful place, great things can happen. In its rightful place, mind is the source of true creativity and true intelligence.

In the sleepwalking state of most humans, the foundation of living is located in the mind—we become top heavy, with a tendency to topple over from the weight of narratives that run our lives. When we trip and fall, we try to pick ourselves up again and wonder where we've gone wrong and how we can fix ourselves and how we can find that elusive and much desired state of peace and spaciousness.

When we live in right relationship to life, in right relationship to ourselves—in other words, when we listen to the innermost, when we meet life as openness—mind comes into right relationship with the totality. Mind comes down off its pedestal and bows to the deep heart. It comes into service of that which is open and awake. This is the right foundation for living. And from this foundation, we come into alignment with an innate intelligence. When we listen to this innate intelligence, we are no longer tormented by mind.

"Does alignment with innate intelligence mean I no longer need a spiritual teacher?"

Alignment with innate intelligence means the inner teacher and the outer teacher become one. This alignment goes beyond the mind's desperate thirst for knowledge to the innermost knowing that is always in touch with what's true for you. And that truth is an inner impulse, like a guiding light in you. When this inner impulse moves you, it goes beyond what might appear to be right or wrong, spiritually correct or spiritually incorrect, enlightened or unenlightened, or any other dichotomy born from the mind's borrowed knowledge. It's an inner knowing, an inner guidance system that is very organic, very natural, and nurtures the cultivation of goodness. And the cultivation of wildness.

What I mean by the cultivation of goodness is allegiance to what is true in you—allegiance to the innermost, tenderest impulse. Even if there is fear, even if there is doubt, even if there is confusion, even if there is discomfort, if you give your allegiance to the innermost, tenderest impulse to move in this way or that way—even when the mind is screaming to go another way or to not go at all—this is the cultivation of goodness. This is the cultivation of all that is whole and holy in you. It is the cultivation of God-ness.

It's also the cultivation of wildness. What I mean by wildness is the vastness of truth. Truth is uncontainable and untamable. It can't be packaged, although spiritual teachings often do try to package it and feed it back to us in the form of knowledge. Truth doesn't conform to expectation or hope or imagination. It doesn't conform to any agenda. This doesn't mean that it is rebellious in the sense of pushing against something—there is no violence in this wildness. Wildness is a true rebelliousness—a rebellious spirit that will not be contained by inherited beliefs or the incessant push and pull of a reactive mind.

The cultivation of goodness and wildness is the marriage of illuminated mind and illuminated heart. And only when the two come together can there be right relationship and right action.

FIVE

Discovering Your True Authority

"The whole purpose of my teaching is to ignite your own inner authority, to help you see where you give yourself away, to show how your need for love or recognition or acceptance is keeping you small. And to invite you to stand as openness in the face of all the world throws at you."

The Marriage of Illuminated Mind and Heart

There is a tendency on the spiritual path to focus on the mind-qualities of illumination—such as clarity, insight, and wisdom—and to perpetuate the idea of an all-seeing, all-knowing God-like state as the pinnacle of self-realization. This emphasis on mind-illumination is prevalent in both old and new spiritual teachings of enlightenment. But a great error is made when supreme wisdom is upheld as the most precious prize. Not only does it keep the carrot of awakening just up ahead and never quite reached, but it also ignores the vital importance of the heart. It is only through the tenderness of the heart that an illuminated mind can flow into our humanity.

The heart is what feels, and feelings must be felt in a direct way—otherwise all sorts of imbalances arise. I'm not talking about the drama of emotions—I'm talking about the tenderest of feelings, those subtle whispers of doubt and confusion and failure and rejection and loss that are inevitable parts of the human experience. Even enlightened beings have a human experience. When this human experience is not admitted, a veneer of perfection gets presented to the world while the heart either atrophies or becomes a monster. This often comes to light through a personal crisis in a spiritual teacher's private life, or through a scandal involving power or sex or money issues in a spiritual community.

Holding-up the enlightened state as some kind of supreme wisdom gained at the expense of tenderness of the heart is no different from the patriarchy of religion or of politics. In both religion and politics, there is mind over heart. There is no synthesis of the two—and in the lack of synthesis we lose our humanity, we lose our true power, and we lose our true authority. We lose our true sovereignty because we hand over our authority to an external projection—an external father figure who we believe will save us, an intermediary between our innermost and God, between our inner knowing and truth. The search for enlightenment often recapitulates that kind of patriarchy.

The time has come to admit to our humanity, so that the mind's illumination can filter into the belly of our earthly experience. I'm not talking about flitting in and out of an awakened state and a human state. I'm not talking about a polarity, a dichotomy. I'm talking about a merging of the two—a true inner marriage.

The heart becomes illuminated when we allow our allegiance to truth to support us in seeing beyond beliefs—beyond concepts or ideas or hopes or fears—to what is truly here right now. It's a cutting-through, a piercing of the veil of projection based on conditioning. When that illuminated view can filter in, through humility and through tenderness, into the depths of who we are, the heart stops being a reservoir of hurt and defense and need, and starts being an open vessel for love.

Now we can start to live with illuminated mind *and* illuminated heart. It is the end of an inner patriarchy, the end of giving our authority over to an imagined power. It is the end of the myth of enlightenment as an elevated superhuman God-like state.

It is the beginning of a new world within you. And the beginning of a new world within you is the beginning of a new world.

An Inner Revolution

"How can I help to change the world?"

True change begins when you look within. Wherever you are on your spiritual journey, you have to begin by being ruthlessly honest. You begin by being ruthlessly honest with yourself about what is *here* in your direct experience, in your inner experience. You begin by having the courage to face yourself totally—not sometimes, not halfway, not just when you feel like it, not just when the conditions are right, but *always*. You begin by noticing how you hold back from exposing the truth of your feelings to yourself because you fear you might be judged, because you fear you might not be good enough, because you fear you might be unloved, because you feel you might not be worthy enough.

Your true power is activated when you see that there is no external authority—only an imagined one. That imagined one is usually somebody in our lives (a father, a mother, a husband, a wife) or somebody from the past (a schoolteacher, a boss), or some "higher power" or "universal consciousness." By seeing that there's no external authority but the one in your imagination, you pierce through the veil of illusion and start seeing clearly. This clarity gives you the courage to face yourself, so that everything that's here—wanted or unwanted—can be included in acceptance. This acceptance fosters a tenderness toward what is here, a kindness toward what is here. Most people want to be kind, most people want to be compassionate. But we most often don't start in the one place where it matters—within, with our feelings.

It's helpful to understand the difference between a feeling and an emotion. A feeling is what is here *before* it becomes an emotion. An emotion is what happens when a feeling has gone (or been driven) underground and built up in intensity, when there has been some kind of denial. Feeling is a *direct* experience, and it doesn't actually last very long. It's like the wind blowing through us, it keeps on changing. As humans, we feel—that's how we experience life. An emotion is much more solid; it has weight and shape and texture, and generally lasts quite a long time (sometimes years!)—until it comes to the surface to be expressed or transmuted. When it does get adequately expressed or transmuted, it becomes a feeling.

Sensitivity toward feeling is what allows the purification of the heart. This purification happens when we stop armoring the heart, stop self-defending against what might hurt, stop denying what might be unwanted, stop protecting ourselves from feeling vulnerable.

Vulnerability is the doorway to openness—and openness is your essential nature. Openness is what you were born as, and hopefully openness is what you die as. Denial of that openness creates suffering. The doorway to that openness is the feeling of vulnerability. We feel vulnerable when we expose the truth of our feelings—when we admit to ourselves that underneath our carefully orchestrated posturing of cleverness or confidence or conviviality we actually feel powerless or unlovable or broken. There can be no acceptance of our humanity if we do not admit the truth of all our feelings, however seemingly dark or ugly they are. And there can be no truth if we are not willing to feel vulnerable in the telling of this truth to ourselves.

True wisdom—wisdom that is truly lived, that is truly breathed, and that has an impact on your life or on anyone else's life—can't be lopsided. True wisdom arises when the full light of truth falls all the way into and through your heart, to the very belly of your existence. This is the wisdom of wholeness. A new world is the birthing of this wholeness in you.

"Is there anything I can do to change my life?"

Instead of asking *"How can I change my life?"* it's more helpful to ask *"What is my deepest longing?"* An inner revolution begins when we ask the right question. What matters isn't so much the question itself, it's where the question takes us.

Usually when we've gotten over the fantasy of looking for fulfillment through wealth or social status or romantic love, we look for it through having good feelings and positive thoughts. We may say to ourselves, *"If only I could always think positively, always think lovingly, always feel happy, always feel comfortable, always love myself, then I'd be at peace, totally fulfilled."* But whether we look for fulfillment in the world of outer form or the world of inner form, we're still stuck in a horizontal dimension.

The real revolution begins when we look deeper, when we start falling into the verticality. If the question *"What is my deepest longing?"* is to have any validity, it must remain open-ended. If you come to a definitive answer—*"It's happiness, it's love, it's finding my true purpose"* and so on—that's a clue that something even deeper is waiting to be discovered. The mind is acquisitive and will come to an answer. It will arrive at something it's sure about, something that will bring the imagined satisfaction or fulfillment it's looking for. But truth is an open-ended investigation in which you are asked to enter the field of not-knowing, to truly listen without a conclusion.

The question—when it's open-ended—takes you vertically, which is the same as saying that it takes you *in*. This movement is a surrender of the mind's pseudo-knowing, a surrender of the mind's tendency to come to a conclusion. It's a surrender of the mind's tendency to find something it can possess—a snippet of knowledge that satisfies, a dream of a brighter future that pacifies, an idea that inspires, or a state of consciousness that gratifies. The willingness for this surrender allows the truth of temporality to be known: that everything that can be acquired with the mind will inevitably be lost, because all things—including thoughts and feelings—come and go.

When the question *"What is my deepest longing?"* goes inward and falls into the realm of not-knowing, it takes you to an openness. And in this openness you are likely to come across all those unwanted feelings that have been tucked away—feelings like shame, regret, abandonment, and unworthiness. It may seem contradictory that the very same journey that brings you to true fulfillment also brings you face to face with everything that seems to be the opposite of that. How can it be that in seeking wholeness you find abandonment? How can it be that in seeking love you find unworthiness? It's because these unwelcome energies are the very portals through which you can discover the power of unbroken presence, an openness that holds it all.

Living from a foundation of unbroken presence is revolutionary. It changes you from the inside out. Your willingness to fall into the groundless ground of unbroken presence means you will die as the "you" you think you are, and be reborn into awakeness. And even if you are alive as this awakeness for one moment only, the revolution has begun.

*"The world seems to pull me away from
my truth. I often feel lost and confused."*

When you finally wake up out of the dream of separation—the
dream of this "little me here" and that *"big world out there,"*
the dream of *"a life that's happening to me, and I have to protect myself or fight it or barter with it or beg it to give me what I
want"* —you will no longer feel lost. When you operate from a
"me here" and *"life out there,"* you are operating in the dream of
separation. Essentially, you have abandoned yourself—you have
moved away from your innate wholeness. So you stop listening
to your true inner authority and start listening to the outer
authorities—the voices in your head, the voices of your parents,
the voices of the politicians or the power brokers or the priests.
You have stopped listening to the truth of an open heart and
have abandoned true knowing for the knowledge you acquire
from the matrix of culture and society. You have become deaf
to the gentle whisper of a wild heart. No wonder you feel lost
and confused!

*"What is the wild heart, and
how can I listen to it?"*

The wild heart is your untamable nature—that part of you which
is free because it can't be captured by anything you think or feel
or do. The wild heart is your naturalness, the innate intelligence
beneath the rules and regulations of inherited beliefs, beneath
the *shoulds and shouldn'ts* of any conditioned mind. The wild
heart is your inner authority—the tenacity to turn toward your
innermost and give it your allegiance, even in the crucifixion of
criticism or rejection or condemnation.

This wildness has nothing to do with being a rebel without
a cause or raging against the machine. It has nothing to do
with saying shocking things or wearing outrageous clothing or

doing a crazy dance. This wildness has everything to do with listening to the deepest truth in you, listening to that which is prior to narrative and prior to reactivity, listening to the silence within—and then moving from this silence. Or not moving at all.

The wild heart is your true heart, before it became obscured by undigested grief and saccharine sentimentality, before it became weakened by ideas of woundedness and encrusted by defenses to protect your vulnerability. Your true heart is an openness that is always here, even when you believe otherwise—an openness that is unshakable, immovable, invincible. Your true heart is *you*—innocent and free.

The Portal of Presence

"I want to become more present. I think this will make my life better. Is this true?"

The idea of presence has become very popular these days—practicing presence, becoming more present, finding presence, and so on. Yoga teachers, meditation teachers, mindfulness teachers, all talk about being more present. It's a worthy pursuit, but when it's co-opted by the self-cherishing mind, it becomes nonsensical.

"Practicing presence" creates a split inside the very mind that's trying to become more present—the mind divides itself. In today's world of spiritual pick-and-mix, presence has become largely synonymous with "not thinking" or "having no thoughts," as if becoming vacant is the answer to all of our problems. But the mind that tries to be more empty is at war with itself—it is fighting against its natural function of thinking. It's like the sky fighting against the clouds.

The idea that you can practice presence is nonsense. You can *try* to cease all thinking, you can *try* to keep feelings at bay, but ultimately you're fighting a losing battle. The belief that drives the effort to practice presence is that if you are successful in being more present, you will no longer feel any pain or encounter any problems in life. But while the practice may bring a temporary sense of calm or peace or stillness, it offers no lasting solution to our human predicament.

Presence is your natural state—it is always here, just like the sky on a stormy day. Only by falling into this natural state can you be fully present.

"If practicing presence is not the solution, what should I do when I get caught up in my thoughts?"

Presence is not an activity from the personhood. The personhood wants to accumulate practices, to make my life better, to make my life happier, to make my life easier, to make my life more spiritual. But this attempt to become more present from the personhood is another attempt at acquisition for the self.

Falling into presence is the falling away of the personhood, the falling away of the mechanism that drives the personhood to accumulate more—to accumulate more knowledge, to accumulate more practices, to accumulate more skills, to accumulate more of something that *"makes me feel better about myself."* Only when that mechanism falls away can you know the true meaning of presence.

Presence reveals itself as the substance of life—as the substance of being-ness—when concern for the movie that appears as your life stops having the primary claim or hold on your attention. When the commentary about what should or shouldn't be happening—*"I shouldn't be feeling this restlessness,"* or *"I shouldn't be feeling this fear,"* or *"I shouldn't be feeling this shakiness,"* or *"I shouldn't be feeling this vulnerability"*—comes to an end, you feel as if you're falling apart because you start falling into the unknown. But it's not really you that's falling apart—it's the ancient mechanism that upholds the personhood and wants to hold it all together by acquiring more practices, more spiritual knowledge, more things to do. When this mechanism starts to crumble, that's a really good sign. Welcome it—it's a sign that presence is beginning to reveal itself. It's no longer something far away in the distance that you have to search for—it's right here under your nose. It's actually even closer than that. It's *in* you, *as* you.

Presence is the solution to all problems—you are no longer a problem to yourself, and life is no longer a problem to you. Aches and pains are not a problem, shakiness or intensity or vulnerability—none of that is a problem. The whole movie—*all* the brushstrokes of life—can move *in* you and *through* you. None of it is rejected. You start to experience the such-ness of life—*just this.* The true happiness you seek is revealed as already here—and it has nothing to do with what you achieve or what you gain or what you know. Presence has no commentary on the content of your life. And without a commentary, there is only the mystery and majesty of being—the innate goodness of this alive moment.

"How do I come to know this presence as my natural state?"

There's an idea that being present has to do with being "mind-ful" —being aware of my footsteps, being aware of this flower, being aware of this *thing* and that *thing.* But it's not in the world of *things* that presence has any real benefit. It's in the inner world of human experience that presence can transform our consciousness and our lives. The willingness to meet your experience *exactly as it is*—whether you like it not, whether you want it or not—becomes a portal to true presence.

Presence is the same as openness. There is an acceptance of

your experience. Whatever it is, it is here because *it is here*. And this *here-ness* is a portal to your true power—the power to be unshakably *here*. Being *here* has nothing to do with feeling comfortable, but everything to do with your innate capacity to bear the unbearable—to fall open into the awareness that is aware of your experience. In this open awareness, you discover that what you think is so monstrous becomes like a child yearning to come home—to be held, to be allowed, to be given permission to just be. This is the deepest acceptance of life that ends the torment of a mind at war with reality.

"Acceptance sounds like resignation. Is there a difference?"

Acceptance is not the same as resignation. Resignation is an indulgence of the "poor me" that's entangled in the unwanted energy. There's a big difference between identifying with the victim and simply being with what is. When you think there's something wrong with what you feel—that you shouldn't be feeling rejected or alone or vulnerable, for example—you become a victim of your experience, a victim of life.

The deepest acceptance has no victim in it. It has no *self* in it. There's no "wrong self" or "right self" in acceptance. Acceptance sees whatever is simply, *as it is*—as energy, as another expression or manifestation of life. Perhaps intellectually you understand this, but the challenge of whether you really do understand it comes when you're in the midst of an unwelcome feeling—when it's actually happening to you

It's right in the midst of that challenge that the doorway appears. The opening door invites you to become aware of the argument that forms itself around the experience and the ensuing hardening into an identity as "victim." When you start to become sensitive to that reaction, there's a possibility of softening the argument, a possibility of relaxing the identity and being tender toward whatever is showing up in you. *Experiment with this . . . see what happens!* What is there to lose?!

The Art of Listening

"What do you suggest instead of the practice of presence?"

Listening—just listening—is a more intelligent way meet reality. And a more intelligent way to relate.

For instance, when somebody close to us—a friend, a mother or father, a sister or brother, a husband or wife—is in pain, we don't often truly listen. We attempt to fix, to give advice, to provide a solution to make the pain or the problem go away. But this is the same as *attempting* to be more present. It's an attempt to find a solution to our own pain, so that we don't have to feel what is truly here. We attempt to bully reality into being peaceful or calm or still or silent, so that we don't feel the discomfort.

When someone is in physical or emotional pain, there is often an accompanying confusion or despair that can't be adequately expressed because it isn't a definite thing; it's an unfixed feeling state that can't be named. When we attempt to jump in with a solution—with an attempt to fix the problem and erase the pain—we don't allow the deeper energetic movement to flow into the open field of consciousness. Everything—every feeling and every energy—yearns to flow out of the darkness, to be fully held in the light of openness. This open field is what we might call true presence. In true presence, there is no avoidance of what is here and there is no attempt to fix. When we truly listen in the open field, we're not bringing judgment or narrative to what is here. We are simply meeting the other in the full mess of what's here, without drowning in that mess.

When someone is in physical or emotional pain and we simply listen, there is a transformation. When we simply listen, without agenda, there is a surrender of the self-cherishing mind that wants to prove to itself that it has the solution or that wants to elevate itself by doing something good. When we truly listen in the open field that is presence, there's a great healing, because we meet each other eye to eye, heart to heart—right here in the mess of the human experience, without trying to push it away or fix it.

There is great power in this kind of listening. We become an "agent of change" —not by trying to change anything or by trying to be anything, but simply because when the mind surrenders its grip on reality we can meet the world as openness. There is no willfulness in this, just the willingness to meet reality as it is. In this willingness, something shifts inside us—the mind's grip is loosened and we fall into true presence. There is no more avoidance or suppression or repression—there is no more any need to escape the bare facts of our experience. Now we can truly listen to reality—we can listen to each other, we can listen to the world, and we can listen to ourselves. We can listen to what is deeper than the jaggedness of the words, to what is deeper than the complaints, to what is deeper than the victim story. What we're really listening to is the silence that is the essence of openness. And in this silence, we are more likely to hear an intelligent impulse, rather than the voice of the self-cherishing mind that wants to fix and prove that it has the answer.

So, instead of looking for more methods to practice presence, it is more useful—and more intelligent—to bring attention to how we listen, to notice when we're not listening, to notice when we want to jump in to find the solution, to notice when we want to avoid feeling our own discomfort. Without the willingness to meet the brokenness of the human condition, there can be no recognition of what's unbroken within it. And what's unbroken, is presence itself.

This presence is not a commodity or a practice. Neither is it a mental state that comes and goes. It is what is always here, available when we stop trying to fix things with the mind. No practice can give this to us—only the vigilance to see how we avoid the bare facts of our experience, and the willingness to meet these bare facts once and for all, can change the way we see things. This combination brings a cleansing of perception that changes the way we meet each other, the way we meet the world, and the way we meet ourselves. The cleansing allows us to see that we are already right here—and that there's nothing we need to do to be more present.

"I'm willing to listen, but my partner is not. He just wants to complain. How do I deal with this?"

Your partner, your mother, your father, your child, your neighbor—they are not your problem. Your story about them is your problem—your being disturbed is the problem. Don't listen to the content of their complaining, listen to the silence in you. When you listen to another or when you listen to the world from this open silence, true relating can take place. Either the other will become more quiet, more present, more open—or they will no longer be drawn to being in your presence, they will move away and leave you in peace.

Meditation

"Do I need to have a dedicated meditation practice in order to awaken?"

To meditate, or not to meditate? The question is a conundrum to the mind that seeks satisfaction. The mind seeks a definitive answer, as if that would bring an end to its unease. The person-hood seeks certainty, as if the certainty of "spiritual progress" would bestow a badge of worthiness or specialness. But the question of meditation can't be answered by the mind. It can only be realized when silence has become the bedrock of your life. This silence is not about closing the doors, turning off the phone, and lighting some candles. Nor has it to do with trying to get rid of your thoughts, or imagining the perfect sanctuary of peace.

This silence reveals itself when you stop giving attention to the narratives that wrap themselves around your experience of reality. This silence happens when you turn toward tenderness every time an unwanted feeling enters your inner landscape. This silence happens when you surrender all resistance to what is. This silence happens when you are no longer the center of your universe, when you have become without a center and the whole universe is in you. Without resistance, there is no inner conflict, no inner division, no outside and no inside, no barrier and no boundary.

When you know your true nature as silence, there is no need to *do* meditation—you *are* meditation. True meditation is a state of being—it is your natural open state. And in this natural open state, there is nothing to move away from and nothing to move toward. You are simply and irrevocably *here*. There is no longer a question—because in silence all questions fall away.

Of course, turning your attention inward by taking time to be still—whether you are just sitting quietly by yourself doing nothing or whether you are engaged in a formal meditation practice—can be very helpful (at least in the early stages) in bringing you closer to the silence of being. But it's not really about whether you meditate or not. It's about whether you can fall into the silence that is always here prior to your ideas of what meditation is or what it can give you or where it can take you. Whether you sit in deep stillness or whether you do something in the world, this silence is always here. It is in you as being-ness. Being-ness doesn't need to do meditation—it *is* meditation.

So, perhaps it's wise to ask a different question—*"How can I meet myself and meet the world as silence?"* This question will turn the mind away from its horizontal searching and call you to the vertical inquiry, where a deeper truth can be revealed.

"So silence has nothing to do with the mind?"

Only when the heart has been opened can we fall into this silence. It's a silence that goes all the way into the very fabric of our being, into the very fabric of our humanity, into our inner environment, and into our outer environment. This silence has no pollution in it—it's not polluted by self-righteousness. Only from here can clear action be taken.

When silence has penetrated all the way, there's really no more need to meditate—because the whole of life is a meditation. There's no more effort required in order to be mindful, no more effort required in order to be aware—all effort is gone. The true meaning of meditation is presence. And you don't need to put effort into being present. You simply are required to meet life undefended—without armoring, without pretense, without the imagination of hope or the imagination of fear.

The invitation to live as silence is not a call to do something as a practice or as a meditation. It's not something you pick up and then put down. It's an invitation to remember that which is always here. You don't have to earn it, and neither do you have to learn it. It's right here—when the mind stops clambering around for something to stand on, when the mind stops clasping to a conclusion about reality.

It is not just in the realm of thoughts that the mind tries to find a position, but also in the realm of feelings. You feel something, and then you're absolutely certain that what you feel is the final say on the matter. You put a label on it— *"I feel sadness"* or *"I feel rage"* or *"I feel despair."* The mind has taken a position.

Then fear arises—the fear that *"I'll be stuck in this feeling."* You imagine this is the worst thing that could ever happen to you. You imagine there's no way through. You imagine you will fall apart. You imagine you're going to lose the happiness or the joy or the insight you had gained. All that is a conclusion the mind comes to, a position it takes. *How do you really know?* The mind just pretends that it knows.

When you meet what is here without imprisoning it with conclusions, a whole new vista opens up. Instead of seeing through the myopia of the mind, you see through the eyes of an open heart. Eventually, this open-ended perception brings you to silence—a silence as which you no longer pollute your world.

SIX

The Art of Being Fully Awake
and Fully Human

"Be wild, be wide, be open. Feel everything, deny nothing.
Reveal your true self to yourself. Be daring enough to be all
of you. Both human and divine. Both Zorba the Greek and
Buddha the Enlightened."

Living in the Paradox

Being fully awake and fully human is the art of falling into grace
while embracing the grit of the human experience. It is how we
know the unbroken amidst the broken—how we dance in the
waves of duality while merging with the ocean of non-duality.

Being fully awake and fully human is not a divided state. It
is not a movement from one state of consciousness to another—
falling into the grace of a non-dual perspective when things are
going your way and you're feeling good . . . and then getting
lost in the duality of internal conflict when things don't go so
well and you're feeling bad. It is a state of wholeness—you are
both broken and unbroken, both fullness and emptiness, both
form and formless at the same time. This art calls us to live on
the razor's edge of paradox.

As long as you clutch at the waves that make you feel high

and resist the waves that make you feel low, as long as you run away from the waves that scare you and chase the waves that soothe you, you have problems in life. Problems in life are not *what* happens, but the conclusions you come to *about* what happens. The problem isn't whether the waves are big or small, whether the waves are gentle or stormy—the problem is *you*. The problem is that you hand over your authority to the waves of thoughts and feelings that rise and fall in you. You believe your thoughts and feelings to be ultimate reality, you believe them to be the final say in the matter.

The fully awake human being welcomes all waves, without becoming any of them. When something good or pleasurable or uplifting happens, let the experience penetrate you all the way. Let it touch you, let it pour into you, let it soak every cell of your being. But don't come to a conclusion about it, or about yourself. When something bad or irritating or painful happens, let the experience touch you, pour into you, pierce your heart. But don't come to a conclusion about it or about yourself.

The knee-jerk reaction—whether we are faced with calamity or with ecstasy—is to identify with the wave. But if you truly want to awaken out of the dream of separation, you must take up the deeper invitation of this wave. The wave invites you to reign in this knee-jerk reactivity, to hold it like you would a wild horse—not tightly with force or aggression, but gently. This gentleness is a gentleness of the heart—the willingness to stay in that tender open space of nonresistance. And there is also a strength in this—the courage of mind to bow down to nonresistance.

As you tame the desire to identify with any wave that comes at you, you will come to know grace through the human experience. Grace is not a special state that elevates you above the human experience—it is simply the absence of resistance to what is here. Grace is what reveals itself when you've let the world obliterate you—not so you are a victim of it, but so you are a lover of it. When you open wide in nonresistance, you become a lover of what *is*.

Being a lover of what *is* has nothing to do with liking or disliking. You are neither lucky nor unlucky because of what's happening. Life is neither good nor bad, neither rewarding nor punitive, because of what's happening. The nature of life is duality—and there's nothing you can do about that. There is birth and death, there is up and down, there is light and dark, there is pain and pleasure, and so on. The waves of life have been coming since the beginning of time and will continue until the end of time—and there's nothing you can do about that. The deepest acceptance of that duality, is freedom.

The more you accept, the more you allow, the more you bow down to life as it appears *now*—and *now* and *now*—as your experience, the more you will fall into a state of such okay-ness, such tenderness, such beauty, such richness and such depth, that all attempts to awaken so as to escape reality will be seen as childish and futile. The only freedom is here and now. No escape, just *this*.

"So freedom is the willingness to live in the paradox?"

The closer we come to truth—and the closer we come to living that truth—everything becomes paradoxical. It is this *and* that. It is human *and* divine. It is messy *and* perfect. It is time-bound *and* timeless. It is relative *and* absolute. It is form *and* formless. Everything becomes paradoxical. In true awakening, we live this paradox—because truth is not an end point. Truth is not an "answer." Truth is not a belief system. Truth is an open-ended-ness within us—and this is where true freedom begins.

The freedom truth brings is not a freedom that negates our

human experience, with all its challenges, with all its ups and downs, with all its losses and heartbreaks. It is a freedom that allows us to live at peace with all of it, even when it's not peaceful. It is a freedom that wipes away all the cover-ups—everything we tell ourselves in order to protect ourselves, to pretend that we're safe, to imagine a perfect destination. It is a freedom that wipes away the layers of defended-ness, all the strategies that we create—mental strategies, emotional strategies, energetic strategies—to get what we think we want from life to feel comfortable, to feel special, to feel loved. But these cover-ups end up being our prison. And there is no fulfillment in this self-created prison.

Fulfillment comes only when there are no cover-ups. It is the fulfillment of internal freedom and has nothing to do with the external. You could be in a jail cell, and still this freedom is available.

Becoming a Master of Life

"How can I function in the world
without get lost in it?"

The true spiritual journey—especially in today's world—requires each of us to become a master. It is no longer enough to seek the master, to sit at the feet of the guru, to worship an external authority. You must *become* the master!

The master is both Zorba the Greek *and* Buddha the Enlightened—a "Zorba the Buddha." A master can dance on the razor's edge of having realized their true nature as unshakable consciousness and yet be fully immersed in a shaky world. A master knows "I am not the body" and yet can function as a body. A master has transcended the ego-self and yet has a sense of self—because without a self, how could he or she function in the three-dimensional world? Without a sense of self, you wouldn't be able to communicate, or cross the road, or go shopping (or hunting) for your food—you wouldn't survive.

So how can you be *in* the world, but not *of* the world?

This question is profound. The solution isn't something you can learn with some methods, by doing a few workshops. To be in the world but not of the world requires a profound inquiry.

It means being willing to listen to yourself from a deeper place—to listen from that place in yourself that is deeper than the acquisitive mind. The acquisitive mind wants to get somewhere, wants to know, wants to grasp, wants to possess, wants to take ownership of its experience. When we don't truly know ourselves, we believe ourselves to be that voice inside the acquisitive mind—the voice that wants to be safe, that wants to be secure. On a functional level—you could also call it on an animal level—we need to be safe and secure. But on a psychological level, this need for safety and security prevents us from knowing our true awake nature.

To listen from that deeper place in you requires such a letting-go, such a willingness to stop giving your allegiance to the voice that drives the acquisitive mind. If you are to live fully awake and fully human, you are required to look within and ask what stands in the way of unclenching the ego's grip on life. Can you tell the truth about your suffering? Can you be honest with yourself about how you fight with your experience, how you make an enemy of your thoughts and your feelings, how you reject and suppress and run away from what you don't like or want? Can you see how, by listening to the acquisitive mind, you are reifying a divided self? Can you see that it's not your experience that causes your suffering, but your rejection of the experience?

And then can you go a little deeper—by asking yourself if you are truly willing to stop rejecting your experience, to stop dividing life into good and bad, to stop making an enemy out of what is here? Because only if you are truly willing to end the war within can you start to wake up out of egoic identity and the dream of separation.

To wake up is to derive no identity from circumstance or experience, and yet to be fully engaged with the human experience. When a living inquiry arises in you—because your deepest longing is to know the peace that is always here whether life's going your way or not—the awakeness of your true nature starts to shine through all circumstances and experiences. This awakeness is a presence that brings you into deep intimacy with life. And only when you are fully intimate with life can there be a real richness to your earthly life.

When you can surf the waves of the human experience—neither spiritually bypassing nor drowning in the mess of it—you become a master of life. What really happens is that the acquisitive mind steps down from its self-appointed position as master. It stops being the one that rules how you operate in life, the one that tortures you, that torments you with endless narratives of rights and wrongs. It's as if this false master dies because you stop feeding it with your allegiance. When you stop believing the voice of this false master to be true, when you stop mistaking yourself for this voice, its role as the "controller of your life" dies—and it falls back into its rightful place. It dies as the tight knot of self, and it falls open into its true nature as being.

In falling open, mind transforms into the servant of that which is true. Now *you* are the master—not as someone who replaces the controller as another "supreme ruler," but as one who has mastered the art of being awake and being human.

There's no passivity in falling open—you're not just "going with the flow," floating downstream sleepily. On the contrary, there is poised receptivity—alertness, vigilance, presence, openness. You are right *here*, unmoving, unshakeable, and yet able to respond to any situation in a nanosecond. You have become a master of life, fully vibrating with aliveness—neither abdicating responsibility nor using your will to overpower life. There is elegance, grace, and a great power in this.

"Does my personality continue to exist after awakening?

There's a tendency to believe that awakening eradicates all traces of the personality. The unawakened mind holds a picture of an "awakened person" as someone who shows no emotion, who speaks slowly, who never refers to "I" or "me," who has no memory of their own past (or at least denies that any personal history remains), who keeps a very straight face and looks you in the eye with a fixed stare, who has no interest in the world, and who shows no frailty or vulnerability.

But awakening is not the death of the personality. As long as we are alive as consciousness moving through form, the personality-vehicle—the very unique mind-body vessel that makes up you as a human being—continues to function. This personality-vehicle is the outer expression of your human life—forged on the anvil of pain, trauma, loss, karmic lessons, ancestral burdens, family dynamics, social and cultural conditioning, and cosmic forces set into motion at the moment of your birth into this earthly dimension. Awakening can't change this fact. In awakening, your messy human expression doesn't just disappear! You don't become an image of perfection, nor do you become catatonic!

What does happen, though—if the realization of awakeness is authentically embraced—is a "flowing into." As formless unconditioned awakeness flows into your life, there is ongoing and never-ending meeting of the light of awareness with the conditioned knots of mind and body. If there is any residue of dark emotions or addictive movements of the mind, these come into the glaring spotlight to be seen—you are given the opportunity to meet them consciously. Of course, it is up to you whether you meet them with gentleness or whether you attempt to force them underground again. If you choose to be gentle toward what gets revealed, there will be a purification. And this purification of the mind-body vehicle is like polishing the surface of a diamond—as the dusty layers of habitual tendencies are removed, the light of unconditioned awakeness can emanate and radiate through you *as* you.

Your willingness to see clearly and to be gentle means that, over time, the personality-vehicle is given to the light of truth. Something dies, yet something is also born—a whole and integrated human being, passionately in love with life yet totally rooted in the absolute truth of essential nature.

"So my unique expression as an individual does not get erased?"

There is a sacred geometry you are born into—call it your astrological imprint, your enneagram type, your human design, your gene-key code, or your archetypal pattern. Call it what you will (or will not, if you are averse to any system of description)—it is an invisible portal through which you enter this earthly dimension, and it makes you uniquely you. Just as the brushstroke of the shape of your face and the color of your eyes are unavoidable expressions of your incarnation, so is the warp and weft of your psyche as it expresses itself in this world.

But everything in the world of form is subject to distortion. Just as cellular function gets polluted by unwholesome lifestyle choices, so can the light of your deepest and truest expression become dulled by an unexamined core belief in separation.

It's like a pristine-clear crystal that accumulates layers of dust because it hasn't been polished. This unpolished crystal is the lower aspect of personality—the unconscious expression of innate traits based on conditioned reactivity.

And then there is the crystal that has been polished—the higher aspect of personality, the transmuted expression of innate traits that flow directly from the open hand of non-reactiveness. The journey of seeking truth, of investigating what's more true than what you believe, of listening to your innermost—all this takes you back and forth from the density of conditioned self to the lightness of being, from the story-maker to the one who is closer than any story. You go back and forth, until by practice— or maybe by grace—you no longer need to go back and forth.

When you no longer go back and forth, a new clarity arises because you become attuned to the innermost impulse of life's intelligence unhindered by the victim-identity at the root of ego's need for self-preservation. Without resistance or cover-up, you are left with the artwork of your incarnation—your sacred geometry. But this uniqueness isn't a set of fixed behavior pat-terns—it's not something that needs to be defended or destroyed, it's not something that makes you feel better or worse about yourself. It is a gentle emanation that flows unimpeded through your life, without taking possession of the qualities that express themselves or thinking of itself as anything special.

Awakening is the demolition of self as story-maker, it's not the end of you as a unique expression.

Light of the World

"Is the world an illusion?"

The world you see is not real—because everything you perceive and experience can only be seen and experienced through your own belief system, through your own conditioning. You don't see a "world as it is," you see a "world as you believe it to be." You see your own divided mind. That world is the "dream of separation" —most people live in the dream, and not in reality.

When the dream is not to our liking, when it doesn't give us what we want or it makes us feel scared or broken—in other words, when the dream is a nightmare—we try to find a way out by arguing with it, by fighting with it, by manipulating it or trying to fix it. Or we try to fix ourselves so we can have a better experience within the dream. Most of humanity is looking for happiness, peace, fulfillment, and love from within the dream—but they can't be found there. They can't be found within the world that we erroneously create from a place of division. Trying to find them there is a futile attempt to find what is real in the unreal.

Jesus said, "The world and its desires pass away, but whoever does the will of God lives forever" (1 John 2:17 [NIV]). What does this mean? It means that the world in which we seek to satisfy our desires, the world in which we seek fulfillment, is impermanent. This world is subject to the law of duality—in everything there is a birth and a death, a beginning and an ending, a rising and a falling, an appearance and a disappearance. Everything that we perceive and experience passes, everything that we grasp with our minds comes and goes. There is nothing permanent in the world—not even our own lives.

And yet the one who does the will of God lives forever. Doing the will of God doesn't mean giving your allegiance to some religious belief. It means giving your allegiance to the mind of God, which is the same as saying "rest in consciousness." The mind of God is the totality of being—the space in which everything is born and dies, in which everything appears and disappears. And this includes you and your experience—you and your life. The mind of God is here prior to your believing yourself to be a separate self having an experience of the world. The mind of God—or consciousness—is undivided. It has no beginning and no end, it has no inside and no outside, it has no subject and no object. There is no birth and no death, no "you" and no "world." The real you—not the one you believe yourself to be—*is* that consciousness!

When you turn your allegiance away from the content of consciousness to the naked reality of consciousness itself, then awareness becomes aware of awareness—and comes to rest in itself. When awareness comes to rest in itself, the contents of awareness still continue to appear and disappear—but you have woken up out of the dream, you have woken up out of the world created by divided mind. And in waking up, you return to the source of true happiness, the source of true love, the source of true peace. You come back to what *is* real. You come back to what is untouched, what is untainted and unharmed by the comings and goings of the world—and the wonderful thing is, the world doesn't have to be the way you want it to be! The world doesn't have to be peaceful or pleasurable—it doesn't have to conform to your wishes—in order for you to return to wholeness. You don't have to wait for a world of harmony or oneness or love, before you can know yourself as that oneness and that love!

"So I don't need to save the world?"

You do not need to save the world . . . the world will save you! The world and its turbulence—the injustice, the violence, the grief, the failure, and the uncertainty—is a potent catalyst for your transformation. What appears to be so dark is really a pointer to the light—it serves the purpose of pointing you toward that which is real. It serves to turn you around from seeking peace or fulfillment or happiness or love from the world you see as outside you, toward the only place where true peace is found—in consciousness itself.

Consciousness is ever-present, in the essential being-ness of your innermost. Consciousness—or being-ness—is eternal, it is not subject to the law of cause and effect. And contrary to what the mind might think, turning toward this consciousness doesn't make you detached from life. It's not that you stand as consciousness looking at life—you don't become a mere witness of life. No. You become one with life—because you *are* consciousness, and consciousness *is* life.

Resting as consciousness, you come to recognize that the world is not separate from you—the world is *in* you. As you deepen into this recognition, there's a purification of the world in you. It's as if you start to ripen—like a fruit on the tree that basks in the constancy of the sun. You ripen naturally—the light of consciousness is cooking you up, so that the fruit can effortlessly drop off the tree. It doesn't have to be plucked or cut off—you don't need to be violent toward it.

At the right time, the fruit falls off the tree. It's like a wine that takes time maturing in the barrel in order to taste good. Or like a chickpea in the pot that needs to be boiled to a pulp so it can then be absorbed and assimilated. Your capacity to be intimate with the world, with all its brokenness—without having a story about the world—is the ripening process. It's the maturation of awakening that allows the light of consciousness to flow through you and into your functioning in the world. True awakening is not about detaching yourself from the world, it's not about rising above the world—it's a natural by-product of having the world totally metabolized and metamorphosed through you into the nectar of love.

You do not need to save the world—because now, *you* are the light of the world.

"But surely we should care for the world?"

Let's be ruthlessly honest here. We think we're so concerned for the world, but we're actually concerned for ourselves! We're frightened for our own survival—if the world is in crisis, if there's a meltdown of economic and social structures, then what does that really mean for *me*? Will I get shot? Will I get bombed? Will I get terrorized? Will I be excluded? Will they take away my rights? Will I be incarcerated? It's all about *me, me, me*! So let's stop pretending that we really care about the world. Let's wake up out of this illusion, because there is no world but the world that is *in* me—the world that I experience—and when I'm dead, this world will no longer exist. Is there someone who will care then? No . . . you only care while you're alive.

The world you know will cease to exist when you're gone, so all you're really doing by caring is trying to hold onto your life. "Your" life is meaningless—it comes and it goes. You give that life meaning by wanting to do something good for "the world." As long as caring comes from the separate self—from the self that believes it has the power to change or control life—it is a pretense. My invitation is for you to drop the whole idea of caring for the world—in other words, die before you die. Don't wait until your death to drop the self and its pretenses.

The world you perceive is such a potent invitation to discover that in you which is unchanging—that which is untouchable, that which will always be here even when all of this passes. The one who is rooted in that which remains when everything comes and goes, lives forever—not as an earthly body, but as the light of consciousness. The consciousness that is being-ness is all that really matters. There is only one being-ness manifesting through all these apparent separate selves in the world—there appear to be billions of beings, but truly there is only one. Discover this being-ness and you will know that which lives forever. Being-ness has no beginning and no end—it is the totality of existence, and therefore it is wholeness itself.

The terror in the world is a representation of the terror in you. The separate self is terrified of not existing and erects a barricade of defense structures to protect itself from this terror— these defense structures are the beliefs and thoughts you have about the world. You believe the world to be this way or that way, but all of this is a padding against the terror of non-existence. You are afraid of death, so you pretend it's not a part of divine plan. You make death an enemy, and you fight for life. But your thoughts and feelings about death and about life are conceptual—they are imaginary.

Discover what is real—face the reality of the body and the earthly experience coming to an end and see what remains. Meet death—and life—in the space of unknowing. This is the art of dying before you die.

Being-ness is beyond existence and non-existence.

"Is there a place for compassion?"

If a movement happens in you from the deepest acceptance, it is real compassion. It is love in action, and you are compelled to respond to that impulse. But if it arises from a place of division, then you are still missing the mark. Before attempting to right the wrongs of the world, you must polish the lens of your own eyes—you must become ever more vigilant to the unexamined beliefs that overlay your experience of the world, that create the story of the world according to you.

"So how does this apply to those in political power who might not have our best interests

at heart, to those who are amassing power for
themselves at the cost of ordinary people? It
sounds like you're asking us to be quiet?"

I don't say be quiet . . . I say be still. Unless you move from stillness—just as a martial artist moves from stillness—there's no power in what you do. Find the stillness within yourself and move from that stillness.

How it looks on the surface—what actions you take, what words you say—is not my business. Neither are they of the utmost importance. It's not about political or social or moral "correctness" —that's all subject to change according to cultural and historical conditions. Right action will arise when you move from stillness, when you move from wholeness, when you move from that space in you that has no self-righteousness in it. This is not ignorance, it's not turning a blind eye or burying your head in the sand. The space in you that's undefended doesn't come with opinions or judgments, it doesn't take a stance.

There is a much vaster reality on a worldly and on a non-worldly level than we can possibly know. There are many hidden factors and influences that are part of the play. There are many engineered events that are a mask for what goes on behind the scenes. And there are many invisible galactic or cosmic or evolutionary forces that weave into our earthly world.

When you find the space of "unknowing" in you, then your actions will have power in them. A deeper intelligence will move in you, and you'll have no choice but to respond from it. It will feel as if you're making a choice, that you're choosing how to respond to a situation—whether in your personal relationships or in relation to a political or economic or environmental situation—but, at a deeper dimension, the intelligent impulse of life is choosing you. You may not be able to change the world, but something *in you* will have changed. And that internal change is what really matters, because from this place you relate to your world from wholeness.

"How can I contribute to the world in times of crisis?"

The real contribution is to be a representative of wholeness—to develop an immunity to fear by resting in that which is deeper than thought. The intensity of collective fear in times of crisis is a thought-virus that marks an evolutionary "bifurcation point" —we are called to evolve or die. By resting in and moving from the deepest in you—from the unshakability of presence and the constancy of being-ness—true immunity is created, mentally, emotionally *and* physically.

Immunity is a holistic affair—all levels of it are representations of each other. Your true immunity can't be taken away from you—this is your invincibility. No thought-virus—nor any physical virus—can enter this inner sanctuary. It's a sanctuary that has no barrier, though, as there's nothing to defend. So the expense of going to war is spared. Your true immunity doesn't start or stop anywhere—but it begins with you.

This is where the rubber hits the road. Has all that spiritual practice and all that spiritual progress made any real difference? Can you stand as infinite openness in the face of worldly collapse? Being "spiritual" is no longer a luxury—it's now a 24/7 job. It's no longer relevant to transcend or detach from the world—we are each being called to make a real contribution, by taking personal responsibility for our immunity to collective unconsciousness. This is the foundation of compassion, and from this place we can take action—we can campaign for justice or be a voice for peace or do whatever it takes to rise as love. Of course, we can't know for certain that this will create the change we wish to see—but there is power and dignity in this, even if the world falls apart.

"What stops humanity from waking up fully?"

The human story is the play of existence. This is the dream, just like the waves that shimmer on the surface of the ocean. Who are we to say that it should be any other way? And yet always there is an invitation to awaken out of the dream.

The mass of humanity appears to be asleep, lost in the matrix of the mind. And then there are those who feel an inner impulse and are compelled to follow the spiritual search for something more true than mind. There are those who have awakening experiences and then go back to sleep again. And there are those who wake up and stay awake. It's all beautiful, it's all part of the shimmering display—we can't make sense of it through knowing.

The attempt to find meaning in any of this—even though it may give us some kind of satisfaction or solace—is a futile attempt to grasp something that is ungraspable. Asking "why" is always from the mind—and the mind is always agitated. The conundrum of why humanity is not yet awake invites us to a deeper layer of unknowing—and it is only from the openness inherent in this unknowing that we can rest in our true nature as the ocean of being-ness.

This being-ness is always here . . . whether humanity wakes up or not.

The End of Spirituality

"Should I cultivate joy and love?"

There's a tendency on the spiritual path to want to accumulate spiritual qualities—such as joy and peace and love and one-ness—as if they were items on a shelf that you can pick up and add to the shopping basket called "my life."

If you want true freedom, this container called "my life" is something that needs to be emptied, not filled up. The shopping basket needs to be cleansed of its flotsam and jetsam, the debris that has accumulated over a lifetime. The qualities of love and peace and joy and oneness are qualities of *being* already in you. But they can't shine through when the shopping basket is full of all the inherited beliefs and reactivity that have accumulated over this lifetime (and perhaps previous lifetimes). These qualities are not objects, but an aspect of the essential you.

There are many spiritual techniques—visualizations, meditations, breathing techniques and so on—that aim to cultivate these higher qualities. These methods may be useful at a certain time of our lives, but if you continue to cling to them beyond a certain point they become they nothing more than spiritual band-aids. It's a little like having a root canal where the cavity is filled up with more gunk, more material to cover up the infection, when what really needs to take place is a deep cleansing.

Discovering your true nature is not a shopping trip. If you really want freedom, you need to empty the shopping basket and then throw the basket away. Emptying the basket requires a "going in" to meet all the defensive structures that uphold your personhood—everything that you think you are. These defensive structures are encountered as contractive knots of energy, the places where we tighten to protect ourselves from being hurt or scared or feeling broken or helpless.

If you go deep enough—if you gently sit inside these energetic landscapes without judgment or interpretation—you are likely to fall into the openness of being. And here, the shopping basket of "my life" is revealed as a figment of your imagination. You see that there is, in fact, no boundary, no container, no ground, and no center—you and life are, and always have been, one.

There is a deep relaxation in this—you can stop striving

to become spiritual in order to live a spiritual life and receive the spiritual "goodies" you think you need. Life is simply as it is—it doesn't assign meaning to itself. But "being spiritual" is something we often assign a lot of meaning.

When the "spiritual shopping basket" dissolves, the division between being spiritual and being human also dissolves. All that remains is the willingness to meet life as the openness you already are. This essential openness is very ordinary—and it changes everything.

When all concepts and ideologies fall away, all that is left is love. You no longer need to cultivate love—you *are* love. The essential openness that you are is synonymous with love—love doesn't interpret experience, it simply *is*.

"So achieving a higher state of consciousness won't help me cope with the suffering of the world?"

This spiritual idea needs to be unpacked—this idea about transcending the world, turning away from the world to go inside and contemplate your navel, achieving a higher state of consciousness in which nothing touches you. All this is simply no longer relevant today.

For a start, you can't transcend the world—you can't do that. It's nonsense. The raw reality is that you are here. You simply cannot escape being here in this experience. Becoming spiritual is not a viable escape route, except in the imagination. You imagine that you can do spiritual things, you imagine you can become more spiritual, you imagine you can make progress on the spiritual path—and you imagine that all this will cocoon you against the pain and horror of the world.

But spirituality won't save you—it will just imprison you. You will become imprisoned by your imagination, imprisoned by your expectations and your striving and your hope of salvation.

There is only one solution to your pain and your problems—to be absolutely present and absolutely open in the midst of the human condition. Not just sometimes, when you're on the cushion meditating. Not just sometimes when you're sitting with a spiritual teacher. Not just sometimes when you feel happy and you feel like being present and open. But always, always, always.

The only salvation is here and now—just this unadulterated presence and unwavering openness.

"What's the point of awakening if there is nothing we can do to save ourselves or save the world?"

Don't be concerned with awakening as a means to an end. Put aside the fantasy of a spiritual utopia. Be concerned only with falling open in the midst of the machinery of reactive mind. Be concerned only with surrendering your weapons of war when all you want to do is destroy. Be concerned only with softening when the tight fist of *"me"* is running through your veins and poisoning the expression of your natural intelligence. You may ask why you should be concerned with this. I will tell you:

So you can stand unbroken in the midst of brokenness.

So you can turn toward tenderness in the face of the enemy.

So you can live as fierce grace when your world comes tumbling down.

A word for this very moment

When I embarked on the journey of offering my teachings in the form of this book, I had no idea the world would almost literally fall apart as the book developed. Certainly the world has always been subject to turbulence, but seemingly overnight it has changed dramatically and many people are facing immense challenges and overwhelming fear in everyday life. I'm often asked in discussions lately if these teachings are of any relevance now.

Yes. They were made for these unprecedented times in which, individually and collectively, we so obviously are facing the unknown. Everyday routines and choices that we long have taken for granted are no longer safe or secure. Our daily habits, our lifestyle, our jobs, our recreation, are all changing. For some there is uncertainty about financial security, for others there is fear around physical survival, and for yet others there is loss of friends and family. The global economy, planetary resources, social patterns, the basis of our health and wellbeing are all on shifting sands. And there is a lot of confusion, a lot of conflicting reports—a lot of information and a lot of misinformation—in the news, in social media, and so on.

But more urgent and fundamental than the changes we see

in the world is the contagion of fear that underlies the unconscious human condition. This fear has always been at the root of
psychological suffering, but now it is amplified because we are
so connected through information highways and world events
that impact us all. Fear actually isn't rooted in the reality of
now. It is the result of coming to a conclusion about the future.
It's what happens when we give our attention to the drama
of thought, when mind flaps about on the surface looking for
something to be concerned with because it cannot rest in the
unknownness of now.

When faced with the intensity of collective fear, we may go
crazy with believing our thoughts to be reality or we may be
forced to go inwards and ground ourselves in what is deeper
than the seeming importance of form or thought. The real question is not how will you cope with your life, but how can you
meet life—*this* life today, not the imagined life, not the future life,
but this very moment—from a deeper place than your habitual
narratives or anyone else's. Can you meet life—*now* and *now*
and *now*—as openness? I'm talking about the very immediacy
of your experience—wherever your location, whatever your circumstances, whatever your state of health, somewhere that is
closer than all of that.

What is closer than economic collapse? What is closer than
social breakdown? What is closer than any loss? What is more
intimate and direct than any thought? Right *here*, right now—if
you stop and *listen*, if you stop and *feel*—is the warmth of your
body, the ebb and flow of your breath, the pulse in your belly.
Right *here*, right now—if you stop and *soften*—is the simplicity
of *being*.

This recognition of the truth of your innermost nature is
not a spiritual palliative. It's not about denying what's going on

in the world. It's not about sticking your head in the sand. It's about meeting reality *as it is,* not as you imagine it to be. It's about waking up out of the dream of separation and returning to the sovereignty of your innate wholeness.

Forgetting our true source as *one being-ness* is what keeps us in a divided internal state and in a divided world. This unexamined belief in a "me" as a separate entity leads to the mass hypnosis of fear and the loss of our true inner authority. But in the midst of adversity is an immense opportunity.

Right *here*, right *now*—is your chance to remember who you really are, to be rooted in that which is more constant than anything that can be lost or anything that can break. This that cannot be lost and that cannot break has been with you ever since you took your first breath and will be with you until you take your last. It is your essential *aliveness*. By aliveness, I mean the naked fact of *"I AM"* that is always here—that can never be taken away from you. No one and no event has the power to take this, your essential nature, away.

So yes . . . my teachings are made for these times. And beyond, because their core is timeless.

A new landscape is before us, a terrain never before traversed. We are called to take one step at a time, gentle yet firm, neither looking backward to how it was nor looking forward to how we imagine it could be. We are invited to befriend the unknown, to get right up close and intimate with an openness the mind cannot possess.

Often we may feel overwhelmed, confused, enraged, as we experience inner and outer worlds crumble and fall. Often we may feel as if we're walking through the valley of death, our hearts broken open and the suffering of humanity pouring in. But as we keep still, perhaps we feel the silent goodness that runs through it all, an undercurrent of aliveness that is always here and so easily missed in the hustle and bustle of everyday life, so easily bypassed by the acquisitive mind.

Perhaps now—in the midst of this uncertainty—we are naked enough to be touched by the impermanence of the world, the insanity of giving our allegiance to fear, the futility of holding onto the known at all costs.

Perhaps now—in the mess of a world shaken to the ground— we are down on our knees enough to be humble enough and grateful enough and kind enough to attend to what is more essential than our cherished beliefs and opinions and ideas of right and wrong.

Perhaps now—as we fall into this unknown moment—we will be resurrected into the verticality of being and walk this new terrain as warriors of an open heart.

Perhaps now we will be rooted in our true immunity of presence, in our true authority as love, and in our true birthright of freedom.

My friend, do not miss this opportunity.

AMODA MAA

OCTOBER 2020

NOTES

1. p. 39 Mirabai Starr, *Dark Night of the Soul, St. John of the Cross*, (Riverhead Books: 2002), 10.

About the Author

AMODA MAA is a spiritual teacher, sharing a fresh approach to the age-old search for spiritual freedom. Her essential teaching features a timeless truth that is highly relevant to this moment—for contemporary seekers willing to go to the raw edge where spirituality meets humanity.

After years of spiritual seeking, meditation, and immersion in psychospiritual practices, an experience of the dark night of the soul led Amoda to a profound inner awakening. Then, after a long period of integration, she began speaking from silence in small gatherings.

She continues to offer meetings and retreats (most currently online), and is a frequent speaker at conferences and events—attracting spiritual seekers and people looking for peace and fulfillment in an increasingly chaotic world. Her teachings do not belong to any tradition or lineage and are accessible to all. She brings to them a deep understanding of the human journey, born out of her own experience.

Amoda Maa is the author of *Radical Awakening* (formerly *How to Find God in Everything*) and *Change Your Life, Change Your World,* both of which arose out of a mystical vision around the time of her awakening. In this vision, she was shown the key to humanity's suffering and the potential for the birth of a new consciousness and world. She also is the author of *Embodied Enlightenment,* based on her vision for humanity and conversations on the cutting edge of spiritual inquiry in her meetings with people from all around the world.

Amoda Maa lives with her beloved Kavi in New Mexico, USA, and inspires a growing following worldwide.

More info about Amoda Maa and her teaching at
www.amodamaa.com

Her videos are available at
www.YouTube.com/AmodaMaaJeevan